THE ART OF BEING GOOD WITH MONEY

Published by TV18 Broadcast Ltd, 414 , 1st Floor Empire Mills
Senapti Bapat Marg , Lower Parel (w) Mumbai 400013

C & P 2019
Cover Image and Book Designed by
The Big Idea Communication

Printed and Bounded by **Print Process**
B-23 Royal Industrial Estate, 5-B, Naigaon Cross Road,
Wadala, Mumbai - 400 031. Tel.: +91 22 2412 0587

Printed in India
First Edition Published in 2019

ISBN 9789387860650
MRP Rs 499/- (Incl all taxes)

For Corporate Enquiries, Bulk Sales & Customer Care email us on bestsellers@nw18.com
or contact us on +91-22-4001 9829/744 (Monday to Friday 10am to 6pm)
or SMS “CD Bulk” 51818

Disclaimer

While TV18 Broadcast Ltd and Network18 Group Companies the promoter of this Book, and the author have taken due care and caution in compilation of information, generation of analysis and provision of expert recommendations appearing on this Book and/or provided to the subscribers of the Book by means such as sms/ Books/ print media or other electronic medium, we do not guarantee that such information is accurate, verified, adequate, current, complete or comprehensive. We disclaim all liability and responsibility for any inaccuracies, errors, omissions or representations appearing on this book or in the information delivered to subscribers by any means/ media. Accordingly, your reliance and action based upon any of the information contained either in this Book or delivered to you by any means as part of this service is entirely at your own risk.

The Views & Opinions expressed in this book are the author's own & the facts are as reported by him, which have been verified to the extent possible & the publishers are not in any way liable for the same.

The content appearing in the book or delivered to subscribers by any means is provided for information purposes only. The viewer/subscriber should independently verify the information before making any financial, trading or purchase decision or for any tax/ legal/ regulatory reporting. The statements appearing on our Book or delivered to you by any means, as part of this service, should not be regarded as an offer to sell or solicitation of an offer to purchase any products.

This Book may contain a number of links to other websites. In providing these links, TV18 Broadcast Ltd and Network18 Group Companies and the Author do not in any way endorse the contents of these other websites. TV18 Broadcast Ltd and Network18 Group Companies has not developed or reviewed the contents of those websites and does not accept any responsibility or liability for the contents of these other websites. Should you use a link from this website to any other website you do so entirely at your own risk.

Foreword

Finance is a dense subject that does not interest most people. Hence, people tend to avoid looking at matters financial or postpone it for a later day and time.

Until I came into the financial planning domain myself, I was bored, even intimidated by finances. Now, being a financial planner, I realize how important it is for people to relate to their finances and have the right understanding. Only this will ensure good outcomes for them in their lives.

It is truly ironical that people work for about 35 years of their lives to earn money but pay scant attention after they have earned it! This cavalier attitude towards finances is the reason for the perilous state of finances in many peoples' lives.

Also, people have many wrong notions which come in the way of their financial well-being. This results in people leading a life filled with stress and worries.

Manikaran is a good friend and my peer in this field. I know his journey – the transition from a banking background to that of a financial advisor. He has shared his journey with his readers so that they may also get some context of where he is coming from.

I find that this book captures the essence of his journey as a financial advisor and seeks to share his distilled wisdom with the public. The title of the book, says it all

The book is about how to approach, relate to money and a good explanation on the relevant areas. I would say it is actually coaching the readers on good money approaches. The book deals with money habits, our ideas about money, pitfalls, psychological traits that affect the way we save/ invest, financial freedom etc.

There is a philosophical approach in the book which appealed to me a lot. Finance is not all math. It is about our life and emotions and Mani has strung the psychological and philosophical aspects well, with the typical financial constructs like asset allocation, risk profiling, budgeting, cashflows etc. That is what I would call a well-rounded coaching for someone with not much knowledge of finances.

Mani calls that Good Moneying! He has been writing a blog by the same name for years now and has been able to attract a steady stream of people, who were looking to sort out their finances and get set for a fulfilling life.

His blog readers will find that this book encompasses his overall philosophy and approach to finances and life, though it may not have gone into each area in as much detail, as in his blog. This book offers the required framework for one's financial well-being, whereas his blog delves deeper into specific areas.

He draws inspiration and parallels from many sources. You will find the wisdom of Stephen Covey in the book when he is talking about character and Sadhguru's pronouncements about one's own efforts and duties. You will find the book peppered with references from Bollywood movies as well, which many readers may find relatable and brings out deep insights in a humorous way. We need all the humour when it comes to finances and Mani has sprinkled some in his book, to good effect!

Overall, this is a well-intentioned book to coach the normal public about finances and gives a well-rounded view from financial, behavioural, psychological, social and family view-points. The book is a quick and easy read. It is not a tome.

This book is like the food which after eating, is still light on the stomach. It informs and educates with a light touch.

I hope readers would find the book interesting and engaging and will be better persons and good with money after reading this book.

Suresh Sadagopan

[illegible]

[illegible]

[illegible]

[illegible]

Preface

I was meeting my schoolmate Rajan after a very long time. He was passing by my city while vacationing in Himachal, and he decided to stay back for 1 day in Chandigarh.

I picked him and his family up from the airport and brought them home. After some chit chat while we were waiting for lunch, he asked me, “So where do you suggest one should invest these days?”

This is a very common question from people who know my profession or when I introduce myself as a financial planner to someone in general.

The question can be different depending on the person’s perception about the current investment market scenario, his beliefs and understanding. It was early 2017 and everything was going great and thus people asked me where to invest. Some even went further and ask specific questions on how to create a “Perfect Investment Portfolio”. Earlier in 2008-09, and even in 2018-19, when the scenario was bleak, people used to ask me if I thought one should invest these days or just keep the money in saving bank accounts or bank fixed deposits. Rather than growth, they were worried about the safety of their capital.

And my answer has always been – “I don’t know” or “Not sure” or “Maybe”.

People ask such questions as per their perception of the then investment market scenario. They believe that what is going on currently is the only reality, which will continue in the future.

In behavioural finance we call it a "Recency Bias" or "Availability Bias". This was the problem in 2003, in 2007, 2009, 2014 and 2018. In fact, every time you need to make any decision about the future, you consider the recent happenings as a base or even your past experiences and beliefs play a big role in whether you go ahead with your decision or not.

You decide based on your thoughts, what you expect or anticipate about the future. How has been your past experience? What is going on in your life at this moment? Your thoughts, your feelings all guide your decision making. As in stock markets, it is said that only 2 drivers drive the market - Fear and Greed.

When you feel happy, you are positive about the future and when you feel sad, your life looks dull and depressing. Your happiness or contentment with your decisions depends upon the outcome you are anticipating from it. Also why were you expecting that outcome...because of some bigger purpose in life or was it because of your feelings?

No one wants to get rich; everyone wants to get richer than others. A job promotion is good, but if your colleague has got a double promotion then your own happiness gets halved and you have all the reasons to justify why the boss made the wrong choice. Our education system has become such that it's no longer about your own good rank, it is more about having a better rank than others. Competition has become a way of life. And with this kind of a mindset and experience when you enter the money game, here again you start competing with others in terms of a big car, a big house, exotic travels, throwing parties, putting children in high end schools...and so on. Coming to my conversation with Rajan, "Goodu, I don't advise on investments just like that" (Goodu is Rajan's nickname).

"Oh, I thought you were into financial planning. Never mind, so what do you do for a living?", he asked.

"I am a financial planner, but for living I do morning and evening walks, sometimes biking too, and if with friends we may go hiking/trekking. I love eating a variety of food and I make sure to explore a new food joint (dhaba, hotel or roadside vendor) every month, and if possible, in different cities too. I love to travel and explore new locations. I spend time with my parents and visit them every month. I am slowly developing a taste for reading and try to read one book every month...and yes I am into financial planning too, and help my clients organize their financials and live their life to the fullest."

"Hey wait!! Seems you have an interesting life. But, the other activities besides your profession, does that make you money?" Goodu was looking bit confused.

I explained, "See, you asked about what I do for my living and this is how I live. For money, yes, I work as a consultant to many families but that is a part of life, as I enjoy doing it. See when you enjoy what you do, you need not separate work life and personal life. My clients are like my extended family and so my work is my extended life."

"So, do you earn well?", his confusion continued.

"Goodu my friend, life is not mathematics. When you look at it in terms of numbers you start doing maths around it. This is what happens when you consider money as the supreme necessity in life. You start looking for ways to multiply the money, believing that more is always better, and nothing looks enough to you. Numbers lead to comparisons, and comparison results into so many different feelings. Such feelings don't let you pause and enjoy what you have. It does not let you look at your life holistically and you find yourself going deep into a rut. I've observed this in many people who number wise are doing well, but still are not happy in life.

All this happens when you do not live your true life and you spend your limited life energy in living like others... your own life becomes all about others. Now that doesn't mean that money has no role to play in your happiness. It does, but only to some extent. Beyond a point you need love, caring and togetherness, it's all about your wellness," I concluded.

This book is about aspects that stop you from living your life, about balancing your life and money. Money is not Life, but a part of Life; yet we spend most of our life energy to earning more and more money, and in the process forget to live Life.

I will discuss money too, as this is the thing that you are trading off your living years for and also ponder on aspects of "the perfect investment portfolio", "how much is enough?", risk, asset allocation etc. but only up to the point where you realize that the rest is all about process, where there is nothing much you can do.

Thus, do not consider this book as a "Get Rich Quick" primer or "Tips to make money faster".

Knowing - Learning - Understanding

Friends, Goodu is not a fictional character. It is you, a Good Side of You (U)!

Every one of us has a good side where we want to live our life to the fullest, do something for society, spend time with our parents and kids and much more.

But since childhood you were told to behave in such a way that you look good to others. Behave properly; study to compete and get a better job than your friends, neighbours, and relatives; then earn more than others, so that you can buy a bigger house, drive a bigger car and lead a happier life.

Your work and income define your status in society...and many more such statements have corrupted our minds such that we have lost our own selves somewhere. All that we do may end up with us having a happier life, but after accumulating so much we forget to live life.

Money is no doubt an integral part of life, but how much is enough is to be seen.

Life is more important. Your life should not revolve around money, but money should be a medium to help you lead a good life. In fact, why just you, everyone has the right to lead a good life and since God has given you the power to earn, so your money should help and support the needy segment of society too. So, make others' life good too. Live good, Create good, Spread good.

This book is to bring out your Goodu! You know what is right and what is wrong, it's just that your mind and your circumstances that don't let you think that way.

Just Like Lord Hanuman was reminded by Jambavan about his powers to fly and cross the ocean to find out the whereabouts of Sita, I too am playing the role of Jambavan through this book to remind you that you too can be free from the clutches of money, and make money your true friend to make it work for your betterment. It should increase the life in you rather than taking the life out of you.

The whole book is divided into 3 sections:

1. Knowing – (Jaano) – Red
2. Learning – (Seekho) – Yellow
3. Understanding/Identifying – (Pehchano) – Green

Knowing is about knowing yourself and finding out the WHY part of your actions. The Learning section is related to money aspects as to how to look at the monetary areas in life and how well to manage it, and the Understanding section is the final impetus which gives you an idea on what is stopping you from moving ahead and how better to deal with it.

I am a strong believer in taking professional help. If something is not your core area of expertise then it's always wise to take an expert's help so that you may concentrate on what is more important. Although I will explain a few areas of money management, it is just to prepare you to ask the right questions and come up with the right problems when you seek professional help.

**Dedicated to
Mumma and Papa**

About Author

Manikaran is a Practicing Financial Planner and the Founder of Good MoneyingTM (www.goodmoneying.com) one of the Trusted and Popular blogs in the personal finance space. He is an MBA Finance Gold Medallist and a Certified Financial PlannerCM.

Having 15+ years of experience in the financial services space, he helps clients across the globe, organizing their financial lives and be good with their money, by offering them Customized Financial Planning solutions and handhold in their complete Money journey.

He strongly believes in Good Money habits for a Great Financial Life, and is on a mission to inculcate the same in his clients, blog readers and the general public by contributing Personal finance topics in Leading Print and Online Media. He keeps organizing various Financial Literacy workshops and Financial Wellness sessions for Corporate employees and Professionals.

He can be reached at

Email mks@goodmoneying.com

Twitter @mksingal1

Linkedin https://www.linkedin.com/in/manikaran/

A Note of Thanks

Three kinds of people were pivotal to this book: the ones who encouraged and motivated me to write; the ones who supported me during the process; and the ones who are behind the ideas and stories written.

But above all, I would like to thank the Almighty because of whom, these three kinds of people are in my life. Thank you, God, for everything.

The first ones are my dear friends Kiran Telang, Hemant Beniwal and Jitendra Solanki. It was Hemant who pushed me to new heights and recommended me to Network 18, then Kiran who helped me get the final yes from the publishers. So, I can say, I am an author now, just because of these guys. Shukriya dosto!

I am grateful to Suresh Sadagopan, who has been a guide and mentor since I embarked on my financial planning career. He constantly surprises me with his insights and solutions to all my problems and answers to all my questions. Sir ji, tussi great ho.

To my office team, Sunny and Varun. Sunny let me concentrate on writing and took good care of most of the office responsibilities.

To Anusha Ramani at Network 18 for accepting the idea of being good with money, which I think is a step above than normal mathematics of financial planning.

To my editor Aditi Radhakrishnan and her new born who I would like to call as Goodu. Actually, Goodu was the one who pushed me to complete the proofreading, so that he could have the complete attention of his mother after coming to this world.

As for the underlying stories and ideas, I want to thank all my clients, my blog readers, the prospects who seek my services, my friends and all the members of the Financial Planners' Guild, India (Association of Registered Investment Advisors) who at some time or the other shared their or their clients' stories, experiences, challenges and learnings and made me ponder more on those thoughts.

Thanks to all my teachers and gurus. They played a very important role in making me who and what I am today.

And to the most important person in my life, my wife Shilpa, who played all 3 roles in writing this book. She encouraged me, supported me and also shared ideas. She was the sounding board in the whole book writing journey. She loves me more than I love her. She knows me more than I know myself. She is a friend, a boss, a critic and everything in my life.

MAY GOD BLESS THEM ALL

Table of Contents

Section 1
KNOWING

WHY BE GOOD WITH MONEY?

WHY BE GOOD WITH MONEY?

Nothing much has changed since 2003, the year when I entered my professional life. I started my career with a private sector bank as a Management Trainee. Besides normal banking, we used to sell investments or I should say insurance policies to the bank's customers, with only one visible feature, which was "High Investment Returns".

I have intentionally used the word "sell investments", because we were not told or trained on how to advise. And when returns are coming, no investor actually bothers about advice. Moreover, this was the ultimate objective of the investor too, and no one was interested in asking anything else. Everyone wanted to multiply money fast.

I was witnessing the biggest bull run of my life, even though at the time, I was not even aware of the meaning of a bull run! You name a stock and it was growing. You invested in mutual funds and saw 30% returns per annum. Some were getting double every year. That was the time when "Har gadha ghoda bhaag raha tha" and it was difficult to figure out which one was the gadha and which was the ghoda.

In 3 years', time, my job performance or I should say the market performance made me believe that I was not meant for a job, and should sell investments on my own. Jitna salary se milta hai, utna to waise bhi kama sakte hai. And selling on your own was the way to make money faster than a monthly salary. And yes, I did very well, at least in the first year of my business.

Everything was going well; in fact, it was perfect. The way every new business person wants to see it, without realizing that vertical growth comes with its own risks.

Only when the tide goes out do you discover who's been swimming naked - Warren Buffet

The stock market euphoria ended in January 2008 with the biggest stock market fall ever, followed by a long lull in the investment markets. In fact, the lull was from the side of investors who participated to their fullest by 2007 but hardly anyone I knew considered 2008 to be the levels to make investments.

Looking closely, one will understand that investment markets were doing their job; this is the basic cyclical nature of them and generally how it works – boom-doom, boom-doom – it was only the sentiments which went down and took the market's level along with it. Now, existing investors were looking for a way out and new investors wanted to wait or were preferring gold over equity.

The year 2008 put me into pause mode. This was the year that showed the real picture. I had 2 options, either I start searching for a job (which itself was difficult to get in those times) or continue with the investment products distribution business, and wait for things to settle down. Somewhere in my mind one more confusion was bubbling whether this was the right way of doing this business.

Those were difficult times. But when I reflect to see what went wrong, I found out that the issue was not in the investment products or markets in general, but something else. Neither I nor any of my clients were following a process. We were just investing for the sake of investing with only one thing in mind. High Returns.

No targeting life goals. No risk profiling. No discussing life aspirations. No direction. No PLAN.

As the saying goes, <u>if you are visiting a new place the first thing you have to have with you is the right map</u>, which is what we were missing. Direction is more important, which was lacking at the time of suggesting or making an investment. Yes, it was not at all the investors' fault, because when the lighthouse is showing the wrong direction, where will the ship go?

So, I first decided to give direction to myself and completed my financial planning certification and started with advisory services rather than just investment distribution.

Advisor sounds like a polished word than Product Seller. And it sounds good even today. It's easy to convince someone when you tell them that you are advising and not selling. But later on, I found out that it's easy to call oneself an advisor, but to be true to this word one requires to put in a lot of effort.

It was no longer about Investments anymore. It was about Money. Money which has its connections with every aspect of Life. Money that brings Comfort and Luxury. Money that brings Peace and Stress. Money that Simplifies as well as Complicates life. It is so ingrained in life that looking at it separately from life would not be wise and thus, although buying and selling investments is important, it plays a small part in the overall financial picture.

Financial planning is not just about writing a plan as I was trained and certified for. I was not aware that it would open up so many other chapters of my clients' life that just working on numbers would not be enough and that I would have to work on many more things. Discussing money with someone requires deep trust, and when you trust someone deeply you not only share numbers but your feelings too.

Below are some of the statements that a few of my clients and prospects have shared with me. Take a look; you may be familiar with some or all of these issues.

- I am doing well in my job; in fact, my promotion is due next month. This is what I always wanted. But something somewhere in me is not happy. I spend 2-3 hours of my day in commuting between office and home and my health is deteriorating day by day.

At the age of 42, I am diabetic and hypertensive.

- I am living a healthy life in the US. The system and administration are far better than India. I earn well and live a peaceful life. But I keep worrying about my parents' health back in India. I can go back to India anytime I want, but then my income would be reduced to one fourth and we would not be able to save much for our financial goals. My lifestyle may get compromised.
- My father did a lot for me and I want to gift him a house of his own. I would like to take my parents on a world tour. We want to live together in our native village. So, I want to accumulate money to the maximum possible.
- My friends suggested that real estate is the best investment which multiplies money fast. Now I have 4 properties and all are on loan. Sometimes I feel the cash crunch. I am also worried what if tomorrow I lose my job.
- My work takes a lot of my time, due to which I can't spend quality time with my family. But earning money is also important. I am unable to balance my work-life.
- Earlier my wife also used to work and was financially independent. But after having kids she had to leave her job. We live away from parents due to my employment. And she does not have a social life too. Now after the kids have joined school, she is kind of feeling alone and I am afraid this may impact her health badly. I am worried. Can we do something about it, like have a goal for her future? Would that be manageable in my limited finances?

- I earn well and support my parents and contribute to family expenses. But post my wedding I am feeling a cash flow crunch as I cannot balance my and my spouse's personal expenses and family requirements. My parents expect me to contribute a certain amount but now it is getting difficult for me to manage for the same. All this is creating stress in my married life. I am feeling depressed.

There are many such stories I keep hearing from my new and old clients. That is the time I understood that money is more of an emotional subject, and money management does not only require analytical or mathematical acumen, but behaviour management too. It is no longer a numbers game.

But on the face of it, everyone wants to hide behind money. They feel having more and more money is the only solution to all their problems in life.

In 2017, I saw the same euphoria I witnessed in 2007. Come 2019, many investors are as afraid as they were in 2008. People still are getting sold on returns, by their "advisors" who are coming up with many different name and titles now. Moreover, with the heavy and ready information flow nowadays, thanks to the internet, people buy of their own accord and not because someone is selling to them.

Goal-based investments are in favour but setting goals is something difficult to figure out and thus the person ends up again with the same old goal of “high returns”. Goals are getting set not by families discussing between themselves or understanding what exactly they’d like to have, but by going on the internet and then deciding what they should have. Rather than talking to each other and deciding on a common goal, couples prefer to ask Google for solutions or look around as to what others are having. They make investments not considering their goals, but looking at star ratings.

This is the age of ROBO advisors. And humans take advice from robots without understanding that the core of the issue is emotional and robo-algorithms do not understand emotions. All this to save costs and earn more!

When you look at your life from only one dimension, which is money, you limit your thoughts to that particular area only and start finding solutions from that source. Accepting the fact that money is only a part of life will help you look at the other important areas where money plays a less important role.

Good Begets Good

You must have heard or read this phrase many times. In school books, in some spiritual texts, may be in some articles or from spiritual gurus or parents and grandparents when you were a kid. It sounds like a simple and normal statement, but has the answers to many of our life’s questions in it. And as money is also a part of life so applying this phrase to money will make your financial life easy and manageable.

Yes. It sounds very simple but simple things are actually difficult to follow and apply. We all want to have a simple life but intentionally or unintentionally we get ourselves into so much complexity that after some time we find ourselves difficult to come out of it. Sometimes the answer to that complexity is also very simple but it's not simple for us to accept that. We have complicated our life so much that getting back to simplicity looks difficult.

So, how does being good apply to Money and Life?

Good is something we expect our children to be; we seek out a good life for our parents and ourselves; we want good returns from our investments; a good bonus, good spouse; and we want everything around us to be good.

The problem starts when we just go a step ahead and without even having achieved "good" we aim for "best". The data on internet searches clearly shows that people are no longer satisfied by good, and they want to have the best, as in Best Investment, Best House, Best Advisor and maybe even Best Spouse! Of course, the attitude is why settle for less, when you can have more. More is always better. And thus, in the lure for more, we ignore what is good and available to us, and do not enjoy the same.

This is important to understand that "best" comes only after "good" and moreover it is nothing but considered to be a better version of good. And as the old saying goes, "Good Begets Good" — you will get good, only when you are good. Be good to those whom you are expecting to reciprocate in good. You want a good life, then you have to be good with your life. You want a good job then you have to be good with your job. You want a good salary, then you have to be good with your work first. Until you respect and be good with what you have you will not get good in return.

We may not be doing bad or harming these aspects of our life, but we may not be doing good either, which is why we are living an average life. An average life is when we just live and not enjoy. A good life is something that we relish.

Goodness is our first nature. It is inherent in us. We always want good for ourselves, and also, we never want bad for others, unless we are competing with others or we have to prove something to some other person or we want to look good to others. In other words, our goodness goes for a toss when others come into the picture. Others can mean not only a second person but also a third. Like Hum Tum aur Woh.

"Woh" is the so-called life and society pressures; "Woh" is all the excuses that is preventing you from being good; "Woh" puts us into comparisons and makes us expect unrealistically. We start living the life that others are living or want us to live, and forget that happiness comes from real goodness in the way we see ourselves living.

If you see success as having something more than

others then you will never be successful in life. It is only happy people who are more successful in life, as they are happy with what they are doing and what they have. You cannot always be happy if your happiness comes from having more of what you have in comparison to others. Happiness comes from contentment.

When we are not sure what goodness is, then we start thinking that good is something better than what others have, or good is something which others do not have. This is where we lose the essence of a happy life.

You may buy a better car, a better house, or find a better job, but it is important to remember that better is always in comparison. If it is not good but better then it must be something which you have not selected, but this is what the “Others” or “Woh” have made you select.

The things that are looking better today, will lose its charm when it gets old after 3 -5 years or may be even tomorrow. Every non-living thing has its own life and it depreciates over a period of time. It has a limited charm and after that charm is over, you again start looking for something better.

But when it comes to relationships, which is where life resides, only goodness plays a part. Sincerity, honesty, integrity and trust are the pillars of a good relationship. And when you invest in relationships its only grows and deepens, unlike things. You cannot buy good relationships; you have to invest in them. And when you invest well it gets better and better. Here better does not mean in comparison to others, but in comparison to yesterday. Relationships with yourself, your spouse, your parents, your kids, friends, colleagues, neighbours etc. all have to be nurtured. Unlike things you just cannot replace or exchange relationships. In a relationship, you just cannot always say that the “fire” is burning out and seek out an alternative or just leave. You have to be responsible and mature towards your relationship. When things are not working fine, take it as a challenge and work on to improve it.

Like many other relationships, money also has a relationship with you.

Just like your child you are responsible for having it in your life, or just like your parents you are blessed with it. So, you have to take care of it the way you want it to treat you.

You have to provide it with options where it has enough opportunities to grow, you have to provide it with enough protection so it and you feel secure. You have to take care of its health so your own wealth can stay healthy; and you have to help others in their need so the universe may reciprocate the same when and if you need it.

You need to guide and protect it like parents, you need to support it like a child. Be friends with your money, so it can help you when in need. Be like a good employer when you want it to work for you, be like a good spouse when you want it to care for you.

All in all, be good with your money. Be good the way you want it to be good with you.

Comparisons and expectations don't go well with your relationships. No one like to be compared and neither does money. Money does not want "Woh" to dictate terms. It wants you to speak with it. It wants you to understand it well, so it may also understand your needs well.

It is the one which provides good education to your kids, enables your healthy and stable life, supports you in maintaining your lifestyle, helps you in thick and thin: so, it carries a special place in your life which also makes you more emotional towards it.

It is a one important thread woven in the fabric of life. But unfortunately, you can depend on it or it can help you only to a limited extent. As the credit card advertisement goes... "there are some things money can't buy."

So, it's good to be good with money, but expecting it to solve all your problems is not wise. And many times, money itself becomes a problem like getting into wrong company. So, you have to be vigilant and manage all your relationships, including money, the way they are meant to be.

Do you think we require money to maintain relationships? Do we require money to take care of health? Of course, yes! But you need to understand how much.

When something is that important in your life, then do you really give it the respect it deserves?

We will discuss more about this in the later chapters of this book.

Goodness is always Inside Out. It's in your Basic Character.

Stephen Covey in his best-selling book The 7 Habits of Highly Effective People coined the term Character Ethic. He wrote that people can only experience true success and enduring happiness as they learn and integrate a few basic principles into their basic character. These basic principles are integrity, humility, fidelity, temperance, courage, justice, patience, simplicity and modesty.

In the lure of getting faster success, everyone works on personality or public image. Our outer self.

People use "How to communicate effectively", "How to be an influential person", "How to communicate well to close sales", and many more such "How to's" as quick fixes for faster results. The influence techniques, power strategies and communication skills are no doubt important to achieve some degree of success but actually are secondary, especially in your relationships.

And when you are so concerned about your personality and are doing everything to look good to the outer world, rather than being good from inside, then you may achieve your goal to some extent but you will never be able to relish achieving the goal. Unless it is coming from the heart, unless it is your primary characteristic, you are trying to manipulate things.

Covey says that these social bandaids and aspirin appear to solve acute problems but that is temporary and leave the underlying chronic issues untouched to fester and resurface time and again.
There is no "technique" that can drive you to real success.

Focusing on technique is just like cramming your subjects in school, which may have gotten you good grades. But until you have paid the price of following a process, and spent good time in understanding the things, you can never achieve mastery of the subjects you study and develop an educated mind.

Only basic goodness gives meaning to technique and makes the success last long for you; and goodness lies in good character.

Benjamin Graham in his book The Intelligent Investor which also is termed as a Bible for investors, wrote that being intelligent simply means being patient, disciplined and eager to learn. This kind of intelligence explains Graham, "is a trait more of the character than of the brain".

Effectiveness, character, integrity and honesty is not important only when you deal with people: your money also expects it from you. As I explained in the last section, money reciprocates the way you treat it.

You have to respect money the way you want it to respect you.

Just like an academic process brings discipline in your kids and takes them from one standard to another, in the same way put your money into a disciplined process.

A "Get rich quick" or "become a crorepati in some years" attitude does not help in nurturing money and this kind of attitude will not bear fruit over the long term. This shows how desperate you are in making money, and desperation is not good for good relationships. It may make you some more money, but this attitude does not show your gratitude towards what you already have. It shows as if you are using money to make more money.

If you are just making an investment, and want to make money fast then you may use some tactical strategy which may work for the short term depending on the market scenario. But when it is about building wealth, preserving and growing it, not for yourself but also for generations to come, then that demands not just a short-term strategy but a long-term process.

In other words, it demands your character not a personality.

The formula of success, be it monetary or professional, requires only 2 things - time and disciplined efforts. Results are bound to come if your efforts are sincere and regular. Discipline requires understanding, process and timely reviews. We will discuss more on this in later chapters.

Disciplined efforts help in building habits, which slowly turns into character.

Respecting Your Money

Respecting your money means taking care of it properly. Your money is governed by how you treat it. Money has a very important place in our lives. If we give her the respect she deserves, she will reciprocate in the same way. Showing respect to money means understanding its value in the true sense. The way you treat the money shows how respectful you are towards her.

A lot of time I hear statements like "Please invest carefully; this is my hard-earned money", or "I want to invest safe with my hard-earned money" etc. when someone is actually looking for an instrument to invest in for the first time. But I have never heard people saying this when they are planning for a vacation, or purchasing goods/clothes at a sale, or going out on a weekend break or splurging on their lifestyle. Does the importance of hard-earned money vanish at the time of spending? Or is it just the way you perceive it?

It is easy to put restrictions and expectations when you hand over your money to some other person but when you are told to take care of it, you take it lightly as it is now your personal property, and you are free to treat it the way you like. The way you treat your money is usually a pretty good indicator of the way you treat yourself. The opposite is also true, as in if you are good with yourself, you will be good with your money too.

Call it a coincidence, but most of the time I see that people seeking financial planning services are somehow already leading a planned life and now they just want their money to live the same way they are living. They are process oriented people, they are health conscious, they are disciplined and they know the importance of goals.

It's not difficult for them to find out and give me the details as to where their money is going, as they keep track of all their expenses or at least are aware of them. They discuss more on the systems rather than products, they are more concerned about goals rather than returns. They are more focused on the future and understand the uncertainties, rather than cribbing about the past and ruining the present.

If you feel that you are among those who actually treat money well, then answer the following:

- Do you know exactly how much cash you have right now?
- Do you know your bank account balances?
- Is the loose change all in one place?
- Do you know where have you kept the bill of the last purchase you made?
- Do you wear all the clothes lying in your closet?
- Do you have an expenses/savings budget in place? And if yes, do you follow it religiously?
- Do you maintain an all-expense file? And if yes, how often do you view it?
- Are your investments all in one place to track?
- Do you invest with goals in mind and with a disciplined approach?
- Did you ever purchase anything when you actually didn't need it?
- Have you ever obliged someone by investing in a product not suitable to you?

If you know how much money you have, where is it coming from, and where is it going then you may consider yourself a bit organized in money matters.

Conversely, if you haven't any idea on what you own and what you owe, this may indicate a life that is a bit out of control. You may keep on wanting for more, even if what you require is already there. You will not value what you have, will not be content with your efforts, but may always feel the lack of something and may keep cribbing of not having much.

We spend a huge amount of our time working hard

to earn what we have! We all spend a good portion of our lives using money and worrying about money. Even those who are born independently wealthy aren't immune to this.

Any money that you have represents a portion of someone's life, usually your own, as you have spent years, months, days, hours, minutes, seconds of your life to earn it. Even if you got it from your parents or someone else it is the portion of their life. So, every time you buy something, whether a physical thing or a service, you are giving up a part of your very short life for that purchase.

What Does It Take to Be Good?

In the cult movie Andaz Apna Apna, there's one scene where Amar (Aamir Khan) and Prem (Salman Khan) follow Uncle (Paresh Rawal), without knowing that the person they were following was the duplicate uncle and a don. Sensing a problem, they wanted to find out why the uncle's behaviour suddenly changed. All this was to prove themselves worthy in his eyes so that he marries his daughters off to them.

Have you seen this movie? If not then you must, as there is nothing more divine in life than a good laugh. The movie is actually a laugh riot.

Now when Amar and Prem enter a building while following Uncle, they are shocked to see him in a bad state, or rather atypical of his true self. Actually, the

Uncle had a twin brother. One was the original Uncle (Ram Gopal Bajaj) and other one was his twin brother and the negative character or Teja.

But this reality was not known to Amar and Prem. And thus, when they reached the place, both saw two uncles with the same face, at the same time. Amar saw an "ayaash" type, who was boozing with girls and other gang members and Prem saw a "bechara" type, who was in a jail.

"Prem – Oooiii Maa!
Amar – Aaila!
Prem – Yeh kya Uncle iss halat mein?
Amar – Yahi to main soch raha hu, ek hi pal mein duniya badal gayi.
Prem – Abhi ache bhale to the.
Amar – Abe, ache bhale to abhi bhi hai...yeh bure bhale kab se ho gaye"

Both of them were looking at Paresh Rawal and were concerned about his state, as both had the same goal i.e. to do good and rescue him, but without knowing the fact that there was a duplicate uncle too. And with this confusion they ended up doing something that further aggravated the problem.

Now, you must be thinking what point am I trying to make?

See, you want to be good in life and have good intentions always, but when life throws you in a situation, which may look simple but has long-term repercussions, then the confusion like Amar and Prem crops up. All this leads to indecisiveness and wrong decision making.

Your heart is Prem and brain is Amar. Both have the same goal (rescuing Uncle) or as in life (being happy and successful); but they both are visualizing life differently. Because of this they have to put an identification mark on uncle's cheek to identify the goal clearly and avoid confusion in future. Remember this classic line? "Teja main hu, mark idhar hai."

I guess this is the reason why today's generation is called as the Sandwich generation.

When your heart says parents, brain says children; as you have limited time available with you, you think it is not possible to spend time with both. When your heart says vacation, brain says promotion; which is why you do not enjoy yourself in both situations. Depending on the perception you have about investment markets, sometimes your brain says investing with long-term wealth creation, but your heart says speculation and fast returns; your heart may say safety, but your brain says risk. All this happens due to 2 reasons: one is when you are not clear what exactly you want in life, and the other is when you are not prepared for different possible what-if scenarios.

Life is never smooth; this is for sure. Even when it is looking smooth then there must be something wrong. It always throws you into some situations that demand some action or decision from you.

Logically your decision should be impacted by your understanding and knowledge, but in reality, it equally gets impacted by your thoughts, past experiences, beliefs or what you hear and see around. And here, emotions come into the picture and rationality may go for a toss. It happens with everyone. Even though I am guiding you through this, it does not mean that I have never been in such situations. It is human to be emotional. But when decisions are important and going to impact your life, double checking pays.

Let me give you a situation here.

You have enrolled your child in the most popular and so-called best school in town. You expect your kids to do well in studies and even co-curricular activities, but still you find that your kid is slow in studies and not doing well in sports and other activities. What would you do?

Would you change the school or try and find the core of the issue to resolve it? You may start attending PTA meetings on a regular basis, keep in touch with the teachers or spend time with your kid to understand what his issues are and be a guide and mentor to him. And what if even after doing all this, you find that that his score has not improved and or has improved but not up to your expectations? Would you change the school now? Or would you go further deeper into the issue? It could be some specific subjects, or a particular teacher or a specific bad experience which is not letting him think ahead. Your child and maybe you too need some counselling.

There are many such instances in life where you experience the mismatch in your expectations and reality. The same goes with money. You should do the research in advance before putting your kids (read money) into the school (investments). You should not change the investment product every time you find returns lesser than your expectation or in comparison to its peers.

If long-term growth is the goal then the law of the farm or law of nature is the process. Your just sown seed will not start bearing fruits the very next day. It has to become a tree which is a years-long process. Your spouse will not deliver a child after announcing that she is pregnant. It is a nine-month process. And in this process, you just cannot sow the seed and forget about it. You have to take care of it through proper nourishment and medications (if required). You have to do timely review and take actions when required, after understanding how the process goes. Similarly, when your wife or you are pregnant, you take the help of expert doctors, dietitians, may be yoga experts, eat healthy and regularly, read relevant material and ask questions to have confidence about the expert advice. But you trust them, and follow them till the end.

When the goal is financial freedom then you should know what actually freedom means to you. Is it having more money and less time or having more time with reasonable money? Your money demands that attention and understanding from you. And you can do justice to your money only when you have knowledge of what you want, and more importantly why you want what you want. And then with understanding, later you will find out how you should go about it. The problem arises when we only focus on what we want, without the knowledge of why we want that and the understanding of how to go about it.

When the goal is to be good, then you have to be very clear on what good actually means. And believe that goodness is already in you only. You may take outside help but ultimately it is your responsibility. Being aware about emotions, and accepting the fact that emotions may lead to indecisiveness and confusion, is the key to actions and asking for professional help. As the saying goes, direction is more important... and for direction you have to be sure on where you want to go.

In the next few chapters I will try to take you through some common financial concepts and how to interpret them for your financial wellness.

FINANCIAL FREEDOM – FIRST ENJOY, THEN ACHIEVE

FINANCIAL FREEDOM – FIRST ENJOY, THEN ACHIEVE

It was January. Winters were at their peak in north India but since this place was near Mumbai, the weather was not that cold. Still, waking up at 5'o clock in the morning was a challenge. But I woke up without difficulty, and not just that, I even took a bath and within half an hour reached the yoga classes. 2 hours of yoga class, followed by breakfast. There was only daliya (porridge), fruits and milk; no paranthas and butter which I was fond of. But I was enjoying every bite of whatever was served. The later part of the day had two naturopathy wellness sessions (pre and post lunch).

The full day schedule was such that it also provided me with ample time to visit the library or the juice bar to sit in quiet and read. There was a meditation hall too, where one could spend time with oneself. In the evening there was again two hours of yoga and pranayama sessions, followed by dinner and a lecture on spirituality.

It was a week spent well at a yoga and wellness centre, in the hills of Lonavala on the Mumbai-Pune highway. I was doing the things I liked to do, I had spent quality time with my spouse (with the mobile phone switched off), I was happy. I was feeling FREE. There was nothing on my calendar, except the yoga and wellness sessions that I loved doing. I could choose what to do the rest of the day.

"Wow!! Sounds great. I must say what a wonderful life you have!" This was the first reaction of some of my friends whom I was sharing my experiences with of the last holiday I went for.

A friend said, while sipping green tea while sitting in front of a room heater, "You can do this Mani, you are your own boss, and you are free. We can't. We do not get 10 days of holidays at a stretch. Even if we could, we may not be able to keep our phones switched off for such a long time. And during our holidays, things keep piling up waiting for us to come back. Moreover, you are a planner, you must have planned well for your life. It is difficult for us who have designed our life in 9 to 5 till we are 65."

I was not sure if he was sarcastic or happy towards me. But it was quite visible that he was disappointed with his life (at least in that particular moment).

I responded, "I must agree with you guys especially the statement you said about yourself that you yourself have "designed" your life you are living. Your life is your choice. And when you talk of planning, it is not always for finances, it is about life too. The way you plan your life, decides the way you live your life. And this is what I am doing, living my life the way I want. Finances are just part of it."

"You mean, we can also live the way we like?" Seema, one of my friend's wives asked curiously. "We can also be free, and may be not now but in the future, we may live a financially-free life?"

I smiled, "Dear, you are already free. See, if you were not free, you would not have been sitting here back biting and making fun of your bosses and blaming the government for all the bad things happening in your life, no?" The group broke into laughter.

I continued, "Ok, jokes apart. We may not be independent, but we are all free. We can either enjoy our freedom or compromise freedom for our wants. It's just that what you do with your freedom is all that matters."

Everyone there was looking at me with perplexed eyes. So, I elaborated further.

"There are 2 things, freedom and independence, which may look like synonyms but are actually quite different in its meaning. Independence is the state when you are not dependent on any one for your requirements, but freedom is a broader term. Freedom is all about mind set. Referring to India's freedom/independence, we got independence from the Britishers on 15th August 1947, but only after a long battle fought by our freedom fighters who were already FREE.

They were free in their thoughts, free in making opinions, free in taking action too. But they were uncomfortable seeing their countrymen not living freely, so they decided to fight for this bigger cause, to ignite the fire of freedom in other people's minds and help India gain independence from British. And that freedom came to them from knowledge. Almost all the freedom fighters were professional lawyers and thus understood law very well. This made them understand the impact of different rules, policies and laws the British were coming up with, and the impact of the same on India at large. It was knowledge that generated confidence in them. And it was free will, that led them to use this knowledge for a bigger cause. They fought for a bigger and better cause. India's independence had become their life's purpose.

And here you are who are struggling with their own lives, who do not even know their life's purpose. Just because one friend has spent a good time on a week-long vacation, all of you have questioned your own freedom." I just tried to ease the atmosphere with this example.

"So, what should we do now? Shall we all leave our jobs and go on vacation to feel free, shall we compromise with the kids 'education? Who will pay our loan EMIs, who will look after our houses? It's all a theory, easier said than done." Rajan (Goodu) said sarcastically.

"See, that's my point." I continued, "What you are talking about is dependency, not freedom. You are still free, but you are not independent. And due to that you are compromising with your freedom. Doing what you like is freedom and liking what you do is happiness.

We all give away a part of freedom when we desire for more. We all are victims of our behaviour biases, which does not let us save and spend properly. The bias of instant gratification makes us buy first and pay later, that is why we prefer taking loans. Home loans, car loans, credit cards, personal loans etc. are all part of life these days. When you are so deep into EMIs, how can you FEEL free? That's why I say, freedom is a choice.

Leave aside loans, look at your kids' education cost. We feel big names mean high quality, and that is why we want our kids to study in posh schools...and to support all this every year we devote our life and compromise freedom and health to earn more.

And this "more" gets so ingrained in our minds that we have started feeling that more is always better. We want more from our employer, we want more from our investments, we want more from the government... and slowly we start asking or expecting more from spouse, kids, parents and even friends.

I believe the two important things that can bring Financial Freedom in your lives are: Knowledge and Behaviour Management."

"And what about savings?" Seema asked.

I responded, "Yes, yes, savings too. But I believe that your savings can never be enough if you do not work on the important aspect of knowledge and behaviour." Let me explain.

How is Knowledge Important in Financial Freedom?

Knowledge is not only about having facts, information, and skills acquired through experience or education; it is also about knowing what to have knowledge about. **As knowing leads to applying the knowledge well and putting it to better use.**

Knowing about yourself, about your needs and wants – When you know what is required, you know what "enough" is. You stop looking at your neighbour and peers. You will know that their needs are different from yours. You will know that you do not need what the advertisers want you to buy.

Freedom is not about buying anything you want; it's about doing anything you like. Unless you are free to do what you want, you won't be able to enjoy the things you bought.

When you can stop doing the things you do not enjoy, that is called freedom.

Knowing that you need to keep upgrading yourself – Learning should never stop. Knowledge brings confidence to face any uncertainty in the job market. Knowledge increases your horizon and increases your employability and independence.

For now, you may be dependent on your employer for your income but you are free to use the same skills where ever you like. Rather than using it to increase your dependency by taking loans, you should work on bringing more freedom into your life, by working on increasing your knowledge.

Knowing that nothing is in your control – You cannot be free, if you are too concerned about what others think of you. Similarly, if you keep thinking about others you will never be free.

You have to learn to let go.

I looked at Seema, "You cannot control your employer, your spouse, your kids, the government, your income, your taxes or your neighbours. What you can try and control is your own self, your expenses, your reaction and responses, your emotions; these are the things which require your focus. This will bring your mind peace and let you enjoy the freedom that you already have."

"Ok, I agree, but what about behaviour? I know my wife's behaviour does not let me feel free at home, but how does it impact financial freedom?" Goodu asked jokingly.

I smiled, "Yes, I am coming to it. You are a victim of your own behaviour. And the biggest behaviour issue besides the instant gratification which I mentioned earlier, which does not let you think long term, is the scarcity mindset. It is not about having fewer resources, but more about a feeling that what you have is always lesser than what is required. See Goodu, if you cannot take a 10-day break from your work, does not mean that you are not free. To enjoy a single day's break may be enough for many.

Scarcity mindset is something that always leads you to think and believe that resources are always scarce for you, which in turn restricts your growth."

I continued, "You keep comparing yourself to others, rather than participating in other's joy, you remain jealous of them; you don't learn from their experiences and hard work but keep cursing your own luck. You don't see the big picture and thus end up making short-term decisions. Scarcity mindset people feel that everything that's needed for future survival and progress is getting scarce or running out. There's only so much of everything available in the world for everybody. If someone does well it must be at the expense of everyone else that's doing poorly.

They are not happy with what they have but are jealous of what others have. They believe in accumulating and stay away from sharing. They always blame others for their own state. For them they are not doing well because of their employer, government, parents, spouse and others."

Scarcity mentality has its reference in Stephen Covey's book The 7 Habits of Highly Effective People where he wrote, "Most people are deeply scripted in what I call the Scarcity Mentality. They see life as having only so much, as though there was only one pie out there. And if someone were to get a big piece of the pie, it would mean less for everybody else. The Scarcity Mentality is the zero-sum paradigm of life. People with a Scarcity Mentality have a very difficult time sharing recognition and credit, power or profit – even with those who help in the production. They also have a very hard time being genuinely happy for the success of other people."

The opposite of this is the Abundance Mindset, which again as per Stephen Covey, "The Abundance Mentality, on the other hand, flows out of a deep inner sense of personal worth and security. It is the paradigm that there is plenty out there and enough to spare for everybody. It results in sharing of prestige, of recognition, of profits, of decision making. It opens possibilities, options, alternatives, and creativity."

I turned to my friends, "Scarcity mindset people look at everyone as competition and believe in the I win-You lose theory, whereas, abundance mentality people want to create a Win-Win situation. That's why the main focus of scarcity mindset people is on costs, whereas an abundant mind looks at long term benefits. A scarcity mindset person finds it difficult to trust anybody, but abundance mindset people believe that to have a healthy relationship, trust is a must. They believe in a Live today and forget tomorrow theory.

Scarcity feeling results in fear...fear of not having enough, fear of losing what you have. That is the reason they are more concerned about the safety aspect and ignore growth factors. For such minds, there are always too few resources to plan. And where there is fear, there cannot be freedom.

Scarcity mindset also leads to more spending. Spending satisfies instant gratification though for a short term. Sellers also take advantage of this scarcity feeling, by using phrases like *Till stocks last*, or *Only 2 left, or Out of Stock, check next week or Buy 2 get 1 free...only for today* etc. These phrases instigate scarcity feeling and let people spend more as there's very less time left or only a few things are available. And the worst part of this scarcity mindset is that it doesn't let people enjoy what they have! Even after getting what others have, the feeling of emptiness doesn't go by. Such people are never content."

"Hmm...I guess I have to agree with you, but how to overcome this scarcity mindset?" Goodu, finally agreed.

I'm sure that you as the reader, have the question as Goodu.

Scarcity mindset is not exclusive to certain people. Every one of us sometimes behaves with a scarcity mindset. That doesn't mean we never behaved with an abundant mind. It's just which feeling overpowers you and at what time. The overcoming scarce feeling is all about ingraining more of the abundant feeling.

You need to be thankful for whatever you have. Make a list of all that you have and see how blessed you are. Look at the positive side of the story. And if you still feel you don't have that many positives then realize that just because you are in a tough place now, doesn't mean that you will always remain in that place.

Learn to share. Yes, the abundant mind believes in sharing. They consider sharing as another form of investing. The more you invest the more you will get. Share your knowledge, share your time, share your money, share whatever you have: you have abundant resources with you. You share your resources with others, they will share theirs with you.

Stop comparing yourself to others: What they are doing is what they value or what they want to do. You do what you value.

Think long term. List down your goals, make a plan or take the help of a planner to structure out how to achieve them. Take your financial life head on. There's nothing you cannot change. It's just that you need to take the first step.

To be FREE, you have to come out of the Prison, which you have locked yourself into. The Prison of expectations, Prison of negative thoughts and Prison of possessions.

They say financial freedom is a stage when you can buy anything you want, without worrying about the money...I say when you are at a stage when you can confidently refuse purchasing more, as you do not need it, that is called freedom – freedom from materialism and consumerism. Financial freedom is a state when you are and feel free to do anything and everything, with the money you have. You don't need to exchange your time for money, but you value your time the most and spend your time the way you want without being worried about money.

But when freedom is something only financially driven and being valued only in terms of how much money you have and you strive only for that in your earning years, then in most cases you are sacrificing your health, friends' and family's time for something that you do not value inherently. This doesn't mean that money is secondary in being financially free, but it's a state when your money works for you and gives you enough time to enjoy your life. As I said, freedom is a state of mind, and you will feel free only when you feel secure. Sometimes you may feel financially free, when you have enough money to take care of your and your family's basic necessities of food, shelter, education; sometimes even after having all luxuries, the insecurity still prevails within you. As a famous quote goes, some people are so poor that all they have is money.

some people are so poor that all they have is money.

Financial freedom may also be called as a state of contentment, i.e. when you are not attached to money and feel content with whatever you have.

Some feel that contentment is the enemy of growth, but I feel that only a content mind can innovate and bring growth. You need to prioritize your responsibilities and desires, and work towards achieving the same. A discontent mind cannot focus on what is important and keeps doubting its ability to generate growth. The more contended you are, the freer you will feel, which results in more growth.

Ask yourself, do you really enjoy your work or you are working just to earn more and more money? Why do you require more money? Is it because you have specific financial goals to achieve or you have so many loans to take care of? Look around you, do you really enjoy what you have or are just after accumulating what others have? You also need to understand that freedom doesn't mean anything if you are not able to enjoy the same. Striving for freedom is fine, but you need to take care of your health too and take along with you the important relationships that you feel are required for you to enjoy the state of financial freedom.

Freedom is something internal, not a comparison. Look at the things that keep you busy, define your own freedom, check out the things that are not allowing letting you to be free, and borrow the freedom by delegating to others, when you want to use your time the way you like.

YOUR FORMULA OF SUCCESS

YOUR FORMULA OF SUCCESS

When I started my career in financial planning, the first few clients were quite easy to handle. Their impression of financial planning was the same as I was having at that time with my limited understanding, and that was "making investments to achieve goals". We decide upon some goals and do some mathematical calculations to come out with some numbers as to how much and where should one invest to have his goals achieved.

That's it. No further questions.

Today I can say that financial planning is much more than that.

One fine day I got an email from Rohan asking my guidance and help in managing his finances. I acknowledged the email and as per the process I follow, sent him a data gathering sheet to ask for his financial details and goals he was targeting. Within a few hours I got the sheet back, a record! No one had been that quick before!

Rohan was in his early thirties and had married 3 years ago. He worked as a Head of Business Development in a multinational firm. The previous year, he was blessed with a baby boy. His wife used to work as an HR manager with a big brand, but chose to leave her job after having the baby.

So, there were 2 major developments in his life – arrival of a new family member and coming down from double income to single income. It was these changes that made him worried about how to cope with the rising demands of life. These were demands that he had not faced yet, but assumed that they would come sooner in life. For now, it was all in the mind. In the list of goals, he had a specific underlined goal which said "To be successful in life".

This was new to me. Until then I had just worked on the numbers but this particular case wanted me to work on something else, and what's that? Even I was not sure.

The next day was 15th August, and TV channels had all kinds of patriotic movies lined up. I also had plans to relax and watch some of the movies back to back.

There was a movie named Border directed by J P Dutta, which was based on the 1971 India-Pakistan War at Longewala Post. It had a scene when Major Kuldeep (Sunny Deol) from Indian National Army and Wing Commander Bajwa (Jackie Shroff) from Indian Air Force meet for the first time and get into a small debate on which side is more important in winning a war – Army or Air Force. The debate ended on an understanding and closing lines by Major Kuldeep, "Hum hi hum hai to kya hum hai, tum hi tum ho to kya tum ho".

It was a kind of a eureka moment for me, as I found

the solution to many problems in this one sentence. This single line was so deep in itself which explains togetherness, cooperation and synergy, all the ingredients required to win a war or in other words bring peace or solve a problem or be successful.

I immediately called Rohan, and requested him to visit me the next day in my office. But before coming, I told him to get me the answer to a specific question which was – “What does success mean to you exactly?”

He came the next day and as expected with no answer to the question. Since he was not sure what he wanted, I drove the discussion to the next level as to how can he say that he is not ‘that successful’ today? He was clearly perplexed, and had some vague idea in mind but preferred to stay silent.

We all strive for success, but do not enjoy it when we get it, since we do not know as to what is that which we want. Or we keep wanting the things others have without appreciating what we already have.

Rohan was doing well in his job, and in this young age working at a level where many professionals aspire to. He was enjoying a happy married life which is also a rarity in this fast-paced world, blessed with a child which again is a kind of success in today’s stressed world where couples are struggling with infertility. I mean there was so much positive in his life but he was still searching for some other success which he himself was not aware of.

If you look around, you will find many Rohans around you. It may be within you too.

Rohan's idea of success was having lots of money, the main reason of him visiting me. And why he wanted to have lots of money was because he was finding it difficult to cope with the new cash flow structure of the family, where he had moved from Double Income No Kids, to Single Income with a Kid.

It's actually natural. Even after knowing the reality that change is something inevitable, we hardly prepare ourselves to cope with it. People are rarely proactive. It is only after things have happened that you start searching for solutions. And to most people, the best solution is always having more money.

This is where I bring in Border's dialogue – *"Hum hi hum hai to kya hum hai, tum hi tum ho to kya tum ho."*

Financial Success Vs. Financial Stress

Your life is not yours alone. There are many stakeholders in it. You also have some responsibilities to take care of. Responsibilities towards yourself, towards your family, towards your work, towards society, even towards money. This is why you play many different roles in your single life in different times. Finances are important but are just a small part of your overall life.

It is important to know that good health, healthy

relationships, and peace of mind and happiness, have an equal role to play in your success. And it is equally important to understand that you cannot quantify success in terms of health, relationships and happiness. That may be the reason of focusing only on money, as you can count it and compare it. And yes, money also plays its role in managing these 3 parameters. But again, how much is required, that's the question.

How much money is required to keep yourself healthy, to maintain healthy relationships and to keep calm and live in peace? Is only money required for all these or are we missing something?

I never use the word success in my practice. I call it having a RICH life.

Without a healthy self, how can you keep your family happy? If your family is not happy, can you concentrate on your work? If your work life is in doldrums, you would be living in stress, which would further impact your own health, your family life and work productivity too. All things are interlinked and to be really successful you have to work on all these factors together.

When you see success only in monetary terms or in professional terms, then you limit your vision to only one area of your life and lose focus on the other important aspects. I have seen people calling themselves well settled but still struggling with their life demands and stuck in their money matters. Well settled for them is to have enough money so that they should not be bothered to spend wherever they want.

They want to have best of the best luxuries in the world, want to go on exotic holidays, want the best education for their kids, want the best location for their house etc. And in the search of the best they don't shy away from taking loans, in fact their so-called well-settled status gets them easily the loan they want.

And here they start with their first step towards financial stress, which they are actually presuming as financial success.

This does not end their search for the best. As when most of their income is going into lifestyle expenses, they are left with very little surplus to save towards important goals and now they look out for the "best" investment products which generates them high returns.

This opens a Pandora's box and they start trying each and every investment which they think can get them the highest possible return. This exposes them to mis-selling too or should I say mis-buying? When they don't get the returns they expect, this further increases the financial stress and the vicious circle goes on.

Rohan interrupted me here, "So do you mean loans are bad to have? Even if they help you achieve your goals, make your cash flow manageable so you may buy big things instantly like house, car etc?"

He quoted his seniors who have built up their assets on loans and are enjoying their life to the fullest. He was of the view that taking a loan and building assets may be a wise choice, and thus one should not shy away from EMIs as it helps in fulfilling dreams. I asked him how many of his seniors he was in touch with who he felt were comfortable with the EMIs and thus not feeling the pressure of earning money to serve the loans. He responded with some 3-4 names. And what about the others, whom you are not in touch with? How are they doing? I asked. "Not sure about them", he replied.

Now, this was the time to introduce Rohan to an important cognitive error.

Survivor Bias

Rohan was coming from a cognitive error called Survivor Bias. He quoted only those seniors who have been managing their loan liabilities well, whereas he was not sure about the other ones, who may have failed or found it a burden, or preferred not taking a loan at all. This clearly shows that he was focusing more on the former, and ignoring the latter. When you focus too heavily on the survivors of a given population and ignore the failures, this is where survivor bias comes into play. We have success stories all around and try to follow in those footsteps.

You will find successful entrepreneurs getting awards and you want to know more about their work style, you want to read and learn how successful investors made money, and similarly many times when you hear someone made a killing in the stock market through future and options you feel that this could be the right approach to make money fast. If the Sensex or Nifty is soaring high then you make an opinion that the economy must be improving, and if a person is honouring EMIs timely then he must be living a comfortable life.

Success always has an opposite side to it. Those stories do not get published anywhere; they do not find any place in some media news too unless it's the season of bad news.

As Rolf Dobelli says in his book The *Art of Thinking Clearly*,

> "Behind every popular author you can find 100 other writers whose books will never sell. Behind them are another 100 who haven't found publishers. Behind them are yet another 100 whose unfinished manuscripts gather dust in drawers, and behind each one of these are 100 people who dream of one day writing a book. You, however, hear of only the successful authors and fail to recognize how unlikely literary success is."

You will find such examples in all areas of life. A successful surgeon may have a lot of unsuccessful surgeries to his name. A popular lawyer may have lost as many cases as he has won. There must be a reason for Warren Buffett calling future and options as the weapons of wealth destruction. Entrepreneurship is a brave thing, but just building a company with an idea to create a brand to be funded and then selling it off at hefty multiples, may nowadays be a lousy idea. If Bill Gates, Steve Jobs or Mark Zuckerberg were college dropouts, it is not necessary that you should also leave your college to start your venture.

I looked at Rohan, "See Rohan. If you can tell me of some people serving loans well, I can tell you of many others who are stuck. If you can show me secure jobs, I can show you many people who got fired from so-called secure jobs. If you can give the names of the start-ups which were successful, I can give many names who are struggling. Getting motivated from such stories is fine, after all these only encourage us to look at the future with confidence and give us the necessary push to move forward. But to be really successful in a particular area where it is important to do what the successful people did, it is equally important not to do what the unsuccessful people did. For that, you need to go deeper. And sometimes when you have done all the right things but are not getting the desired results, this is where you need to learn that you can only control the process and efforts, but not the results. The bottom line is failures can also give you learning to be successful. Don't just focus on the survivors. It's a Survivor Bias trap."

What is Success?

Success, though has a broader meaning: even if you look at it from a monetary perspective then too it is not limited to having more money. But it is more about using the money on the important things in life and being comfortable with its use, without being burdened.

Money does play an important role in getting you the success you desire, but are you treating the money well for the satisfaction it has given you or are you still craving for more, without showing it the respect it deserves?

Even with money, the parameters for success need to be defined well. You may call yourself successful:

- When you can buy your desired car without even thinking of a car loan
- When you can go on exotic vacations without converting the expenses into EMIs and worrying about your next month's pay check
- When you can comfortably pay towards your parents' medical expenses or even fund their travel without stressing your family budget or disturbing your personal financial plan
- When you are aware of your spending patterns and know what have you spent, where and why
- When you spend time on improving your employability rather than hopping jobs to find a suitable/higher paying option

- When you know that in your absence your partner will take care of money matters confidently
- When you know that the education you are buying for your children will make them a good human being besides a good professional
- When you know that even if your income flow gets interrupted, arrangements are available to take care of important expenditures
- When you know and can balance your life well and give enough time to your health and personal development
- When you come home on time without carrying your work along with you, as this is your family's time
- When people refer your name to their friends and family members as they trust you completely

The definition of success moves around money, knowledge, honesty, health and family. However, the definition of your success is something you have to come up with, keeping in mind the role and responsibilities you play in your life. One should never compromise on honesty, health and family to earn more money. Without knowledge and honesty, you cannot build trust and gain a good hold in the business, profession or job that gets you income. But along with income you also need time to spend with your family, as this is what brings happiness in your life automatically.

Success is not about achieving something, it is enjoying what you have and being comfortable with it. Success is all about doing good in everything you do. It's just that you have to identify the success in you, your life and appreciate it. Gratitude is the best attitude.

Happiness, positiveness and proactiveness, all are the symptoms of success. In other words, you may say that success is a feeling. It's about feeling good. Your feelings come from your thoughts, which result into action. Good thoughts lead to good feelings, which guides you to right actions and thus results into success.

Now when you have identified your "success", the real challenge starts. Maintaining success is far more difficult than achieving success.

Everyone wants to grow in life, make more money, earn promotions regularly, reach new heights in work life, stay healthy. Believe me, making money or getting a promotion may sometimes get easy but maintaining the same is very difficult. In the same way, everyone wants to lead a healthy and happy life. Happiness is a state of mind, once achieved it is something that needs to be maintained by positivity. Health is important to keep going. Getting married is easy but keeping yourself and your spouse happy is difficult.

That is why I say the success is in the process.

Success is not about being RICH, it's about Living RICH. Richness should be reflected in different aspects of your life. And the formula of success which I am sharing here with you in this chapter, will make things easy to understand and achieve.

Success is in the Process

Now I am going to share with you the formula of success, which you've been searching for so long. I have applied this formula on myself and I am getting good results. I am sure this will work for you too. Whichever way you define your success, the formula of success is the same...you just have to change the ingredients.

As I have mentioned earlier, success can mean different things to different people. Some define success in monetary terms, some feel that success is all about spiritual enlightenment or emotional stability. For some, success is about keeping happy, healthy and living a stress-free life, while some relate it to workplace promotions and appraisals. Now in planning terms, would this be fine if I call your definition of success as the goal you want to achieve. For example, if your idea of success is to have enough time to spend with your loved ones, without being worried on the income part, and then this is the goal you want to achieve, right?

In another way, we can call success as the achievement of a goal or something that makes you happy. That goal can be financial, emotional, physical or anything you wanted to achieve. So, here is the formula which we financial planners usually use to find out many financial answers, yet the same formula fits in every slice of life.

The formula of success goes like this:

$$\text{Future value} = \text{Present Value}\ (1+r)^{n} \quad \text{or}$$
$$\text{Success} = \text{Efforts}\ (1+\text{results})^{\text{time}}$$

Let me first explain the components of this "formula of success".

- **Future value** means what you want to achieve or what is your target. Future value is your success figure, which may or may not be monetary.
- **Present value** is the efforts you put in to achieve the desired results. If success means being best at everything you do, then this clearly calls for more efforts.
- **R** is the return you get on your efforts or it is a factor of how fast your efforts are converting into results.
- **n** is the time i.e. how much time you have or give to your efforts to reach the goal.

In financial terms, "future value (FV)" is the monetary figure targeted to achieve, like for retirement, children's future etc. "Present value (PV)" is the money you invest, "r" is the return you get or expect and "n" is the number of years you keep your investments for or stay invested.

The problem with financials as well as personal life

is that you focus more on "r" rather than "PV" or "n". In reality r (rate of return/result) is not in anyone's control but efforts (PV) are. You have to respect time (n) in your life and the sooner you learn this, the more favourable results you get. The more efforts you put in and that too on a regular basis, you will definitely get better results even with low returns. If you focus only on "r" then you are bound to make mistakes.

I was watching a YouTube video of Sadhguru of Isha Foundation, where a devotee asked him what is the most important thing which will lead one to succeed in life - fate, god, luck or effort. He very beautifully explained that all of them are required. But whether you will succeed or not, it all depends on which area you put your focus on. Fate, God and Luck is something not in your control, so they will keep playing their roles as and when they have to, but what you have in your control are the efforts. So, you keep doing your efforts and let the other things be. In the Bhagwat Gita this is called as Nishkaam Karma, which means keep doing the work, with no expectation of returns. Success is the by-product of efforts.

In financial terminology, we call it a compounding effect. A continuous effort for a long period of time creates a compounding impact on the results. This works in every field of life – for example, you cannot lose weight just by dieting, you have to work out on regular basis too, you cannot become a graduate by just entering the college...you have to put in efforts in study. You should not expect a promotion the same year you start a new job...you have to perform regularly and give time to it.

Here 'n' is the most important factor. It results in compounding of returns. More the 'n', better would be the results, in any form you want to see it as. Like if you start inculcating family values in your kids from their early years, you will find them to be a better human being when they grow up, just like if you start saving early for your retirement you need to put in lot less money as time(n) is on your side.

Keeping the returns constant, it is clear that if you have a longer time frame then you can start with a small but regular and consistent effort, whereas if the time frame is short and the goal is big then you have to put in more efforts to achieve desired results. As they say there's no short cut to success and you have to earn it with your efforts.

Define your goals, figure out what you have to do to achieve that, give your best efforts, plan out your strategy, devote yourself to your goal and follow a process. If you are consistent in your efforts, you will surely compound on blessings, love, happiness and yes on money too.

But as they say you cannot get everything in life so you have to settle down at some point and many times compromise with some of your goals. And sometimes your success parameters are so subjective that you won't be able to quantify that. But this should not stop you from making efforts.

Always remember, success comes to those who take actions.... if your PV is ZERO, you should not expect FV.

3 Things Required for This Formula to be Effective

Clarity: The most important thing required to make this formula effective and to keep your life on growth path is clarity. Clarity on what you want and why you want it. You should be clear that what you want is something you desire and not because of something you have seen others have. And if it is the former then what change it would bring in your wellness.

Cooperation: Since your goals are not only yours and there are many stakeholders in it, so it should have others' approval and participation too. You need others' support to help you live a successful life. Relationships are instrumental in helping people succeed: relationships with yourself, spouse, children, friends, colleagues, etc. Good and healthy relationships result in good cooperation and support from them in helping you achieve your goals. Negative or broken relationships have damaging effects on our health, personal happiness, and life expectancy.

Consistency: As I mentioned, achieving and maintain success is not a one-time activity. You need to put in regular and consistent efforts to achieve what you want, to maintain good relationships so that they keep supporting and cooperating in your path of growth and also to gain and regain the clarity on what you want and why you want it.

We will discuss about these in detail in the last chapter of this book.

Section 2
LEARNING

WHERE YOU ARE AND WHERE YOU WANT TO GO

WHERE YOU ARE AND WHERE YOU WANT TO GO

I am going through many emotions as I write this book. In fact, I never thought that I would ever write a book. I never planned to be a blogger or a financial planner in the first place. Sometimes I think that all this happened by chance but when I try to connect the dots, I realize that it was not merely chance but the result of concentrated, focused and disciplined actions that I took but was not aware of and not directed to the place I am at currently.

I never knew what I wanted in life. Coming from a modest business family in a small town of Punjab who spent most of his childhood with his father in a shop, by procuring orders, managing supplies, issuing bills, collecting payments, I never gave any thought on what I would like to become in my life.

Still, to others it was obvious that I would be taking care of my family business. My father had his own share of experiences and was quite frustrated with his wholesale medicine business and thus wanted me to become a banker. He wanted his son to have a comfortable yet growth-oriented lifestyle and for in his mind banking (nationalized banks) could provide me that lifestyle. Although I had heard of some alphabets which I could do after doing B Com which was CA, CFA, CS, but my life had its own plans so I went for an MBA.

In the second year of my MBA, my professor asked me about what 6-week mandatory project I wanted to work on and I replied, "Something on banking". So, he told me to do a survey on the awareness of the Narasimham Committee on Banking Sector Reforms among new age bankers.

Banking was so ingrained in my mind that when corporates came for campus placements in the university, I did not participate in any of the interviews as there was no bank among them. And it may be hard to believe, but in those days, I was not aware of even the "B" of the banking. It's just that my father wanted me to be a banker, and I did not have any kind of direction or guidance, so I thought that banking was "the place" I also wanted to be at.

Finally, I got a job in a bank in 2003. My father was very happy and so was I (I guess). It was a big private bank. The kind of bank we read during MBA as a universal bank where I would be exposed to deposits, loans, forex and what not. So ok...yes, a bit of excitement was definitely there.

It was 25th September 2003, when my professional journey started. Or you may say my working life started, because now when I understand the meaning of being a professional, I can say that my job demanded me to be everything but professional. It was only at the time of the annual appraisal or a customer complaint, that the question on professionalism raised, otherwise it was all about sales, sales and sales.

I was into branch banking, in an extension counter of the bank. We used to take care of normal banking operations like cash deposits/withdrawals, demand drafts, account opening, servicing etc. but since those were the days when the bull phase of stock markets had just begun, we slowly started receiving targets on selling ULIPs, mutual funds, IPOs, bonds and many other investment products.

The bank had some e-learning modules on these products which it wanted employees to clear to improve on the learning, and since I was the only one in the branch having a finance background, I was told to spend some time on it and clear the modules - not only mine but also for all the branch employees! It was on the Branch Operations Manager's performance target list.

After clearing this, I was designated as a product champion of investments in my branch and then I was labelled as kind of a one-stop solution for all investment queries. I had to take care of the branch's servicing, selling and target achievement of investment products.

The targets were big, competition between branches was severe and thus performance pressure was huge. We were supposed to achieve targets at any cost. Sell like FD (fixed deposits), pitch like RD (recurring deposits), don't ask for the investor's requirements and fit the same ULIP for every requirement of the investor. All these were untold ways to achieve high-pressure sales targets.

And I can now say that even investors did not mind investing even after looking at the high cost of the products as they were shown the recent past returns, and were made to believe that this trend will continue.

But deep down, I was not happy. I started doubting the way of advising or making investments. Though everyone was making money - the seller, the buyer, the product manufacturer - I had seen my father working hard in his business and he used to tell me that earning money is not an easy thing in business, which was why he wanted me to do a job. So, I could not reconcile myself to this fast pace of multiplying money.

This was the first time in my life that I gave thought to anything. Anything ever. Earlier my parents used to do this thinking job for me. Even my education or employment was their choice and I just swam with the flow, but now things were different.

The idea of universal banking shattered, I started looking for a new job and gave some interviews in different banks. But everywhere the same game was going on. Unlike Mahatma Buddha, who started meditating under the Bodh tree to find answers to his questions, the internet came to my rescue. And I started spending some time in internet cafes after office hours. Yes, at that time I did not have the privilege to use internet on my mobile phone.

So, on searching for the answer to my doubts, "What is the correct way of making investments" or advising investors, I came in touch with the word "financial planning" and later "certified financial planner". Within a month's time I enrolled for the course and I still remember how I used to travel to Delhi every weekend to attend the classes of different modules.

This was something that truly excited me and I was very passionate about. Without even telling my dad, exactly 3 years after starting the job, I quit. 25th September 2006 was my last day.

At that time, I was totally unaware that I had chosen a difficult path, as investors were not used to being advised. They wanted products that could give them high returns, that's it. The right or wrong way of investing was not their concern at all. Investment meant making money fast, with no consideration given to the goals at all.

But since this time, I was so confident that what is right is right, and this should be the way forward, I decided to give it my all and started on another tough journey.

So, how does my story matter to you anyway?

See, my whole point is that where you are today is because of where you have been, what you have done, the choices you have made either consciously or unconsciously and because of the different people who were involved in your journey. It is because of all the learnings, un-learnings, understanding, ignoring, experiencing, not experiencing in your previous years that you are where you are. And that has everything to do with what is going on now in the present moment... and this present moment can include this very second and/or the current time period in your life.

Your choosing to read this book may be because of your habit of reading that has been developing over years, or your interest in personal finance (which again may not be an instant development) or your following of my blog or any other reason due to your long association with either finances or me.

I am sure that this is not the first book you have ever read in your life time and if it is, then this is the start of building up your reading habit.

The way of bringing up your kids, your way of treating others, your business dealings ...all that you may think of is connected to your experiences and understandings from the past.

So just like I have told you my story, though condensed, you must have your own story. I am an average person, a common man, so I believe that 99% of people around me are same, and they can relate to my story with their own challenges, I am sure.

I have never met anyone who was so clear in his life from childhood on what he actually wanted and also got what he always expected. Most people go with the flow. It is life that teaches them and with the impressions they have from their childhood years, they interpret life's teachings.

Where you are, may not be who you are

Your employment does not define your real worth. Your unemployment does not make you unwanted, your weight does not make you unlovable, your 6-packs does not make you respected. Your scar does not make you less beautiful. Your car, house, your bank balance does not tell who you are, which is much more important than where you are, to figure out where you want to go.

But in reality, most of the time you derive the meaning of your existence in the work you do and the life you live.

When somebody asks you who you are, your first response starts with your name, then with your profession, then your strengths, achievements, and sometimes with family details like your parents, your spouse, your children. This is how you write your résumé and your profile on social media to tell the world who you are...right? This way you define the different roles you play in your life. Boss, employee, team member, husband, wife, mother, father, son, daughter, friend...and so on.

Besides this what you do not consider while defining

yourself is that you are a citizen of a country, you are a tax payer and above all you are a human, which is a very important part of your identity. The former two you realize only when you are asked to deposit taxes or have to travel overseas, but the latter you get to know when you interact with your loved ones, when you feel something, when you love, when you imagine and create.

You being a human has a very important role to play in understanding and learning about your life and even money matters. Humans are emotional beings. You and I have feelings. Our feelings at a particular moment, in a particular situation, are the reasons of our actions. Your investments, expenses etc. all bear the weight of your feelings.

A rich farmer in Punjab writes to the Electricity Board to send her an electricity bill and cancel all the subsidies she is entitled to, as she feels sorry for the state of education and medical facilities in the region and wants the government to use these taxes for the upliftment of these areas. She feels that the government should work towards the upliftment of marginal farmers who struggle with basic necessities.

A retired government servant, every alternate day, clears the litter in the park where he goes for a daily morning walk. No Safai Karamcharis were appointed by the administration in that area. He is of the view that when the park is used by him or other people, then keeping it clean is also their duty. Administration can support facilities but the public should not be dependent on this support.

What made a RICH farmer who is enjoying different kinds of subsidies, paying no income tax and living a comfortable life, feel about the other fellow marginal farmers' standard of living? What made a retired government official, who is comfortably living on his pension, enjoying free health and medical facilities from government, think about the cleanliness in his environment?

To me it is only 1 word i.e. Goodness. Your goodness makes you feel for others, makes you responsible to others. It is your goodness that makes you care about others. And this goodness comes from humanity, which is not something you learn from somewhere, but ingrained in you by birth, because you are born human.

Who you are from inside is what will define your core personality or I should say true character? The way you deal with difficult circumstances, the way you behave in good times, the way you react in bad times, how you treat your elders, how you guide your children, how you value your time and money, how your employees look at you, all depict your character. Yes, I understand in some circumstances you just have to work on your personality to get work done from others but in the long term it is your character that defines your personality.

It is your goodness that makes you a dependable friend, a lovable husband, a caring father...all this defines who you are.

> *"Personality is to outside what character is to inside."*
> ***– Stephen Covey***

These anecdotes appeared in some section of "The Tribune" newspaper. I shared these stories with some of my clients. One of them said, "Mani, these are the stories of well-to-do people. They have achieved what they wanted to, like having lots of money, enjoying comfortable retirement and now they are doing what they like to do. We have many other things to look after for."

"Like?" I asked him.

He replied, "Work and family."

I answered, "See, being responsible does not only mean doing some social work or fighting to bring change in the society. It all actually starts from home. You are already doing your work. If you are taking care of your family, bringing up your kids well and teaching them family values, helping them learn to respect elders, women, friends, taking care of your parents' health and wellbeing, then you are indirectly doing good for society. This way you are not being a burden on society and nature, in fact you are kind of sharing the responsibility of bringing healthy, well educated, sensible people into the system."

Every role you play in life has a responsibility attached to it and when you work with that in mind, you get to know the WHY part of life.

Our roles bring responsibilities along with it and our emotions make us feel, accept and act on those responsibilities and find the reason of living, the meaning of life. The roles which you feel more responsible towards encourage you to act on them first, but when you consider other roles to be equally your responsibility, then that results in confusion and brings inertia. And thus, here comes the role of prioritizing, balancing and above all planning. But all these aspects take a backseat when you are engulfed with other human feelings like that of fear, inferiority, arrogance and superiority, which do not let you move forward.

All these feelings crop up when you forget your basic nature of goodness and start comparing with others. You start asking from others rather than giving. You think from only the scarcity angle even if you have abundance around. This puts you into a rat race and you end up being in a rut and are never satisfied with the life you have.

It is important for you to understand the real WHY of the things you do, by knowing who you are.

Start with WHY...Compete with Self

To define goals, knowing who you are, why you want, what you want it after understanding your roles and responsibilities you play in life is important. The WHY part of the process is the leadership quality. It lets you imagine how you want to see yours' and others' future and even the present to look like. It makes you proactive which is the foremost quality in decision making.

WHY is the meaning to your life. The reasons to your actions.

As the saying goes, he who has a WHY to live for can bear almost any HOW. "How" is the management part of process. The way you live to achieve the "Why". "Why" comes from inside, from your core feeling of being good and doing good. But when it is coming from outside as in being better than others or doing better than others, then the whole purpose of getting meaning is defeated and you get into a competition with others, which leads you nowhere.

You need to understand that there are many "Others" but only one "You".

Your WHY is yours alone, it should not be to please others and does not need any validation from others.

I can understand that it is easier said than done in today's kind of world, where there are fewer jobs than applicants or fewer college seats than aspirants, so competition has become a part of life, and sometimes it's not that bad too. As long as you are competing with your own past, you are competing to be better than yesterday.

When you compete with others, you always see the gap and want to cover that up, and you may find yourself at the low end or high end, which may lead to the fear of being left behind or the arrogance of being in the higher position. And you will never be happy and content. But when you compete with your old self then you will always see the gains as becoming better and better always.

> *"The way to measure your progress is backward against where you started, not against your ideal."* – ***Dan Sullivan***

The feeling "fear" is your enemy; arrogance will take away peace.

Do good, work hard and systematically to achieve your goals, with understanding and planning, but do not let the results or other's reactions impact you in any way.

HOW is the breaking down of the problem, the analysis, sequencing, application and monitoring.

And WHAT is the action at the ground level.

Your Money Life

Money carries an important place in one's life. It is like the blood flow in one's body. Just as blood supplies oxygen to body parts and has a number of other functions that are central to survival, in the same way adequate money flow helps in keeping one's financial life healthy. But just like high and low blood pressure are dangerous to physical health, similarly more or less money may also impact negatively. Also, to have its proper meaning in the body, blood flow needs the heart, kidneys and other body organs to do its function properly; similarly, money is not the only thing that leads you to a financially healthy life. Family values, good health, relationships, togetherness, love, etc. all are also important for a happy life. But to maintain all of the above, money also plays its role.

To keep yourself in good health you have to have money to eat healthy food, do exercise, go to the gym, etc. To maintain good relationships, you have to spend time with them, give gifts, travel, attend and participate in family functions, all of this involves some money,

In other words, money and life go hand in hand. Both are interdependent on each other. Having a good life requires money and money can be earned well if you are living a good life. But if you start treating money as life, and do not take care of other aspects then some day or the other you will realize that "Zindagi ki talaash mein hum, maut ke kitne paas aa gaye."

Where Do You Want to Go?

Before going further, I would like you to take a pen and paper and start writing your own story. How has been your childhood, your adolescence, your school days, college days, work years? Write something about your parents, your friends, your teachers, your colleagues, your boss. Even one line is enough.

This is just to understand their importance in your life. If they are important then how well do you know them? What good and bad memories do you have about them? Did you learn something from them? Not doing something that they did is also a learning. If you do not like someone then that should also be a part of this story and also mention why you don't like him. Just pour your heart out. If you do not like writing then talk to someone, your spouse, your friend, sister or brother.

In routine life, I have seen people cribbing about the bad happenings in their life and they keep blaming others for their present. The major culprits in their life are their employer, the government, the neighbours etc. Many people have played their role in your life movie. Some acted as supporting actors and some were not that supportive. But all had some role to play which is why your life has been exciting. Emotions, drama, action...all are required to make your movie a hit worth watching.

It is because of them that you have learnt to play your

own role in the way you are playing it.

Accepting them all and being grateful for their roles in your life is very important for you to learn and move forward. So, when you write your life story mentioning the people around you, do not forget to mention a note of thanks to them. These are your people, your experiences, your learnings, which no one can take away from you.
These are your life assets because of whom you are who you are. Your present is the result of all of them who are in your thoughts. Your future depends on what assets you own, so use them wisely, and treat them with respect. Even if they are not on the positive side of your thoughts and experiences, say thanks to them.

As the saying goes...gratitude is the best attitude.

- If my dad were not so convinced about banking, I would not have experienced it.
- If my mother was not so caring about my health, I would have studied science and may not be doing the great work I am doing today. It's not that science is a bad subject but it is not my cup of tea.
- If my brother did not tease me about my stammering, I would not have gained confidence in public speaking.
- If my employer was not so pushy on sales, I would not have tried to learn better ways to do it, and be a good advisor.
- Thanks to my parents and my teachers because of

whom I have learned to study and think.

- If the internet café person was not so accommodating, then I would not have spent time studying the options on other financial services, after my late working hours.
- Thanks to God for bringing all these people into my life.

This is also the first step in understanding your financial life too. This is how you write your net worth statement. A statement which will tell you the picture of your current financial standing.

Net worth = Assets (what you own) minus liabilities (what you owe).

Positive net worth is when your assets, your belongings are more than your liabilities.

Your financial assets include your bank balances, investments, real estate, gold etc. and your liabilities include the loans that you have to repay.

Net Worth Statement

Net Worth Statement			
Assets	**Amount**	**Liabilities**	**Amount**
Liquid Assets		Home Loan	
Bank Balances		Vehicle Loan	
Liquid Funds		Education Loan	
Financial assets		Personal Loan	

Cash value of Insurance policies#		Gold Loan	
Endowment^			
ULIPs ^^			
Fixed Interest Investments			
Bonds			
Fixed deposits			
Debt Mutual funds			
Equity Mutual funds			
Direct equity			
ESOPs			
Others			
Tangible Assets			
Real Estate			
Other Alternative assets			
Personal assets			
Primary Home			
Vacation Home			
Car/Vehicle			
Gold / Jewellery			
Other Personal Assets			
Retirement Funds			
Provident fund			
Superannuation			

Gratuity**			
Public provident fund			
Cash value of pension Plan			
Total assets		Total Liabilities	
Net worth = Total Assets - Total Liabilities			

In life's net worth statement there is nothing called liabilities, but responsibilities. What you own are your assets as you have learned in the above section and what you owe to them or to others are your responsibilities, which you have to honour. If you treat them as your liabilities then you will keep blaming others, but when you understand them as responsibilities you know you have to show care, respect and do what is best to honour them. Or you may say these are the goals which you want to achieve. Even your financial liabilities can be your goals as you have to repay your debt at the earliest.

How to Set Your Goals?

How do you want to see your life movie talked about by the artistes involved? Do you want your movie to be critically acclaimed or commercially successful? Or are you not concerned about it at all, as you believe that you have done a great job and others' opinions do not matter to you in any way?

Who do you think would be at peace in the above 3 cases?

These are the main questions which you have to find the answer to. Decide whether your life is for others to judge and be commented upon or you want to live it on your own terms by providing a satisfying and comfortable journey to all the passengers.

As I wrote in the previous section, you play many different roles in your life and each role gives you some responsibility or goal towards it. For some you require money, but for others you require time, energy and skills. Whatever it is, you have to define it first, in your own language, in your own mind to your complete satisfaction.

- How do you want to see yourself in future in terms of your health and profession?
- How do you want your children to remember you as a father? A rich guy who used to buy them lots of gifts but hardly available to play with them or a caring, loving and dependable father who spends time with them, and was always there when they needed him the most and also provided them with a comfortable life.
- How do you want your spouse to look at you? A money machine or a responsible, loving and caring person?
- How do you want your friends, your colleagues to

remember you in your absence?

- How do you want your parents to think of you as a son?

All these would be your explanations. The things that you want to strive for, the things that you want to excel in. You have to be true to yourself first and decide what is that good you are expecting in your life and by being good (in your own terms) you will be able to achieve it. Being true to yourself and knowing what you want is very important, but openness and involving all the stakeholders into it is also important to make your journey smooth.

Remember- *"Hum hi hum hai to kya hum hai, tum hi tum ho to kya tum ho"*

If you believe something is right for your children then you also have to make them understand this and make them part of the process. If you are doing something for your spouse then you have to let him/her know, and explain the why behind it, so you both can be on the same page and support each other in the process. These are stakeholders and not "Others".

Now comes another exercise:

Take a note book and divide the first few pages of the book into 5 sections/ columns.

Give a title to each page with the role you play, as in **who you are.**

Then in the second section, write the name of the person for **whom you feel responsible.**

Third section is to **define what you feel and want to do for that person** as mentioned in the second section above. Put it in a paragraph, in points, whichever way you feel like. Don't limit yourself to space; this is your note book. Extend the section if you want.

Fourth section is for **why?** Here you need to give yourself a reason for the things you have mentioned in section 3. This is the most important section. Do you want your son to study in a particular school or college because you want to show off to the world, or since your friend's children also study in the same school or do you think the school is the one to make your child a better human being? Introspect on your feelings and note them down. Is this because of fear, greed, jealousy, arrogance, an inferiority or superiority complex? Shun those negative feelings and think rationally. Do it only if it makes you truly happy from inside. Negative feelings come from comparisons and you do not need comparisons because you are unique.

The last section is to define **how** you want to achieve the **why**. What does it require – your money, time, energy or skills? What would you ready to sacrifice to achieve this? Would it be better achieved by doing it yourself or by outsourcing?

Let me use myself as an example:

Who am I – A noble soul (This is what my wife says to me when she is in a good mood!)

To Whom – Manikaran (self)

What do I feel about myself and want to do for myself?

Here I am writing about myself. So, think about whatever you want to do for yourself.

My blood reports are showing signs of danger so I have to be cautious and give time to my health. The work life is quite stressful, and these days most diseases are lifestyle related. So, need to keep check on my emotional health as well.

Yesterday, I shouted at my mom. I shouldn't have done it. After all she is my mother. And she is worried about my health too. I think I have started taking my parents for granted. They care for me, but what am I doing for them? I should spend time with them. Get them regular health check-ups. Go on holidays with them.

Yes, holidays are one thing that I love the most. Would like to give myself a quarterly holiday, and an international holiday every second year. There is so much to see in this world and I do not want to spend my life in office surroundings. And I feel holidays are the only time I spent quality time with my spouse, so it becomes more important for me that way.

My work requires me to remain relevant. Things are changing fast. Investor expectations are changing, I need to learn more on the behavioural side of investments so I can keep my clients on track and help them understand the real meaning of goal achievement.

I am very fond of watching movies and eating different kinds of foods. Though my health restricts me to try different delicacies but if I keep my health in check then I would be able to enjoy a variety of food.

Why do I want to do what I want for me?

If I keep myself healthy, I would be in a better position to take care of others. Also, I would not feel dependent on others. Life would be more easy, happy and peaceful.

My parents are my responsibility. They have spent a considerable portion of their lifetime taking care of me and now how can I say that I am too busy for them? I love them.

I feel alive when I am on a holiday. I learn a lot and make new friends while travelling. It gives me a pause, a break from routine, it refreshes me.

Nothing is certain in today's scenario. Updating myself is very important in this ever-changing world. To keep myself useful to my business and clients who trust me with their money I should also understand my responsibility and learn things which may be helpful for myself and client.

Please note: You may find overlaps in some Whats, Hows and Whys...and that's completely fine as in life you are not only you, you are we/us.

How do I want to do it?

1. **Health** - Give at least 1 hour to my health daily. Morning or evening. I don't think I can spare time to go to the gym as its too crowded these days so I would prefer to start morning/evening walk, plus do yoga and practice meditation. Stretching exercises would also help keep me healthy and manage stress. They say that if you walk 10,000 steps daily, you would be away from many illnesses. Will focus on this too.

   What it requires – Time/Money/Health/Skills – All 4, with more of time, and less of money.

   What's the plan – If I get up 1 hour early then I think I could manage it. Or keeping traffic in mind I have to leave from office at least 2 hours early. Need to manage my office timings and work on the efficiency and productivity part of my work.

   As I don't give much quality time to my wife, I

can plan these walks along with her. I need to learn more on meditation too, I read somewhere that meditation even for 10 minutes daily helps a lot in managing stress. And even yoga for half an hour daily has lots of benefits.

I may plan one holiday in a year to some ashram in south to learn more on these and how to implement in my regular routine.

I will start from tomorrow and learn other things in due course. The more I think it over, the more I procrastinate.

2. **Parents:** Visit my parents every alternate weekend with the kids. They love their grandchildren and love spending time with them. Need to get their health check-up done, every quarter. I may also plan to take them on holiday breaks with us. This way I can club my holidays spending time with them. I will tell my kids to go and spend time with their grandparents. Afterall we have also learnt a lot from our grandparents then why should our kids not enjoy this opportunity?

   What it requires – Time/Money/Health/Skills – Time + Health+ Money

   What's the plan – I would have to work on the cash flow, as holidays with parents will increase the total cost. But it's ok. I will do away with some of the weekend breaks and try to cut down on unnecessary outings. Need to follow a strict budget.

3. **Holidays** – Would like to strive for 1 holiday per quarter. May be short breaks. 1 break I would like to have with my friends and the others with family.

   What it Requires - Time/Money/Energy/Skills – Time + Health+ Money

   What's the Plan - I can make a list of places I would like to visit in a year and estimate the travel cost. Or I may start with a fixed budget and arrange my holidays within the budget.

4. **Profession** – Need to keep myself relevant in the industry and to my clients. Would like to do certification on life planning skills. Capsule course can be done online but for detailed understanding I may have to go to the US for a month.

   What it Requires - Time/ Money/Energy/Skills – Time + Health+ Money+ Skills

   What's the Plan – Need to work out cash flow. Business planning is also important as I will be out for 1 month.

Do not Rush

The above exercise may look time consuming to

some. But believe me it is going to be life changing for you. You will be giving time to your life and aspirations. It gives you the opportunity to pause and introspect as to how you can make your life more beautiful.

The same exercise you have to do for the different roles you play and for whom.

Who am I	To whom	What do I feel about and want to do	Why do I want to this	How would I do it? What's the plan and what does it require?
Noble Soul	Manikaran (Self)	---	---	-----
Pepsi/PJ (Pati Ji)	Shilpa (Spouse)			
Manniye (Son)	Parents			
Mani Sir	Office staff			

Financial Goals

You will surely notice that when you answer the question "What it Requires", time and health is common in many goals. Now that is something you have to manage as that is your personal domain. Even skills are something you have to gain. But when money is added to the mix, then that becomes your financial goal.

Money is always in limited supply and there are different requirements for different goals. Some may be regular and ongoing and some may come after a particular time frame. Look at everything from a holistic point of view by looking at your financial picture in total.

Here you may have to take a financial planner's help, who will help you sort out your financial puzzle. Don't ask from Google, don't look at social media, TV channels or blogs. Your life's questions do not require a 2-minute answer. It needs to be valued, and given enough time to understand.

Please understand that you are human and an emotional creature. You may compromise a very important goal for a not-so-important one just because of your emotional weakness. A financial planner is a third party who will objectively view your money matters and help you decide rationally.

It's just that you have to do a trade-off here i.e. gain time by paying the advisor and borrowing his skills or spend time on gaining the skills to do your financial planning. Now you may utilize your saved time to gain health or skills required in your profession, which will further make more money or save money from getting spent on health problems.

I too have a financial planner, as I know many times, I look at my goals emotionally and many behaviour biases come into play even when deal with my money matters. So, it is important to have someone by your side always. It is also important to ask the right questions to get the right answers. And one objective of this book is to help you be prepared with the right questions.

BUDGETING AS AN AWARENESS EXERCISE

Money Feelings/Emotions/ Behaviour Awareness

It was the month of May. The summers had just begun, but the temperatures were soaring. Every other person around me was going on vacations but Rajan (Goodu).

Kiran was already travelling to the UK for 3 weeks. This was the first time she had gone for such a long vacation. Hemant had his own plans. He was trekking somewhere near Manali for 10 days. Jitendra did not have any plans but after knowing about the others, he made his own and now next month he would also be going to the UK of India (UttraKhand) for 2 weeks.

These 4 friends were chatting on the WhatsApp group. Though Rajan was wishing everyone happy holidays, but somewhere at the back of his mind he was feeling a bit left out, as to why he was not going somewhere. Actually, he never plans to go on holidays in June. He believes that when everyone is holidaying, all the vacation spots are crowded and he does not feel comfortable and relaxed, so he always goes on vacation in December. And they (he and his wife) do their budgeting keeping that in mind. But when his reasons were so clear, then why did the news of every other person vacationing bother him?

Just to calm himself down he thought to have a look at hotels in nearby locations, for a weekend break. So, he spent some time on travel sites, and killed valuable office hours. But the real game started afterwards. While searching for hotels, he found a deal which was giving him 50% off, only if he books through a mobile app. So, he downloaded the app, but later found that due to dynamic pricing the price of the hotel was raised to 25%, to give him a discount of 50% and that deal was available for 1 hour only. He was going through mixed feelings: to reserve the room or not, that was the question.

Web sellers had done their job; they created a scarcity for him by limiting the deal to 1 hour, and he was also showing the signs of being a victim to social proof. But this was not all, now that the travel app knew that he was searching for hotel deals, it pinged him with a new offer or other similar places for holidaying every single hour, and tried its level best to tempt him to spend. Though on the face of it, Rajan was trying to avoid the temptation, but somewhere at the back of his mind, he wanted to go on vacation. When he went online to check his emails on the laptop, the travel site followed him. At every nook and corner of every web page he opened, he could see the hotel deals. It was really difficult to ignore those advertisements.

The web intelligence was doing its job, but he had to do his. He had 2 options in front of him: go on a short vacation as a weekend break by buying any of the deals, or control this urge and stick to the plan of a December holiday, which he wanted, had been planning for, and was more likely to enjoy.

At this moment another behavioural issue “Instant Gratification”, played its role, which made Rajan think that what if he could not vacation in December. He started making up scenarios and excuses until he finally surrendered to his desires and booked his weekend break holidays.

So, what do you think this started from?

The core of the issue was his feelings, which was either a fear of being left out or a kind of envy of his close friends. All this came from comparisons. I have always found comparisons or competition or looking outside not inside is the core of many of the problems. If he had a clear understanding on why he was saving for his annual vacation trip, then he would have saved much of his valuable time and also would be able to appreciate what his friends were doing and be part of their joy, which would have in turn made him happy too. By the way, can you guess what he did in December? Yes, he went on vacation then too, since this was what he wanted. That time again his feelings overpowered his mind, and he convinced himself that “Holidays ka mazaa to December mein hi aata hai”. So, in the end it is clear that his expenses were bound to increase, just because he listened to new wants which arose by looking outside and not inside.

Let me illustrate with another anecdote.

Even after attending around 2 months of physiotherapy sessions, Sanjay was not finding much relief in his backache. One thing he could figure out was that this all was the reason of his continuous sedentary work and lethargic lifestyle. Earlier, although God had given him enough signals of his weak lower back, he kept ignoring it by taking pain killers, and now when the pain had become chronic, he could not find a solution. A friend suggested morning walks or running to bring some activity into life.

Sanjay accepted the idea, but then found that he didn't have "suitable" sneakers. Though he had sports shoes, somehow he did not find them good enough, making unique excuses, like he needed a soft sole, or the shoes were not that airy, or it smells too much, or it does not have that "new" technology which is good for back pain while walking.

All this made him visit a store where the sales person showed him the kind of variety he was searching for, which actually complicated the decision-making process. Now in front of him were running shoes, walking shoes, trekking shoes, biking shoes, football shoes...and what not. To make things more complex, Sanjay wanted shoes that would look good on him, good with his tracksuit and with his chinos while going on Sunday office outings or travelling with family. Besides shoes he also found new track pants, water bottles, biking gears, sunglasses, helmet, pedometer... which all just had to be in his wardrobe to start off on his new journey of "morning walk" or "jogging!"

Looking at the stuff he bought, his wife also decided to do the same activities and decided to make their son active too. After all who doesn't want a healthy life (or new exciting stuff!)?

Now after spending almost two hours in the shoe shop, Sanjay and his family had 3 new pair of shoes, 3 new matching track pants, water bottles, and some other accessories in his cart, but while totalling the expense, he found that he didn't have enough money with him to buy all this stuff. Again, the shopkeeper came to the rescue and suggested that he pay through credit card and convert the amount into an EMI, plus if he buys more stuff, he will get some discount too. This sounded a perfect idea to Sanjay, and with this he felt there would be less financial pressure on him so he bought 2 more t-shirts.

Do you see how his not 'understanding of his basic requirements', or 'desire' to have new shoes or I would say 'back ache' or going back further his 'lethargic lifestyle' has put him into debt? Now he will be paying EMIs for the coming months. If you find Sanjay's story a bit exaggerated, then please open your home almirah and find out the reason you have given yourself for buying all the things lying there.

There is a name to this disease, it is called the "Diderot effect". This term was named after the French philosopher Denis Diderot, who in an essay explained how buying a new dressing gown put him into debt, by creating a spiral effect leading to over buying. That one gown led him to buy so many other "new" things just to complement the gown. This effect has been very effectively explained by Hemant Beniwal in his book Modifying Investment Behaviour. All of us are victim to this effect and Sanjay's was just another story, where the idea of replacing his old shoes for new resulted into a big lot of shopping.

Sonia's story should strike a chord with you.

Sonia got promoted to Branch Manager with a salary raise of 30%. It was an achievement for her and she was not expecting such a big raise. Her hard work had finally paid off. Now she could have the lifestyle that she always aspired to by looking at her bosses. Now she could go on international vacations, move her daughter to a better school and have a bigger and better home. She informed her husband Ashish and they decided to celebrate. They planned a dinner date at a five-star restaurant which they had never been to and which had always been one of their dreams. They knew that it was going to be expensive, but they were calling this as a "one-time expense", and with this raise in income they deserved such a treat.

On the dinner table Sonia presented Ashish with an exclusive watch, which he had been wanting for quite long, but could not buy due to money constraints. Sonia's first month's salary raise had gone completely into this purchase only. Over dinner, they decided the next steps of their life. They wanted to replace their car which suddenly started looking small now, get a new big LED TV, replace the sofa set and what not. They weren't just daydreaming, and in the next 1 month it actually happened. Sonia bought herself a new car, and the same month she also replaced the sofa sets, without realizing its impact on her overall cash flows. With these 2 expenses itself, she brought herself back to the same cash flow situation which she was at before getting promoted. Now with these new and ongoing rising expenses, the cash flow situation was such that she skipped her half yearly car maintenance, compromised on her vacation trip which her daughter was looking forward to, and started looking for ways to evade tax to have enough liquidity. Besides this she also started searching for a new job with a higher salary.

Can you relate to these stories or have you heard similar stories in your circle?

The way you spend shows your relationship with yourself, others and your community. Your feelings guide your behaviour and in turn impact your habits. If you feel good about yourself, confident with your own self then you also understand that no car, sofa or TV can add anything extra in your life, whereas if you feel inferior then too nothing can add anything in your life.

Feeling is internal and looking is external. When you say that you want to look good, then you mean in the eyes of others. This sometimes means that you do not feel that others think good about you, so to look good in their eyes you keep on buying new things. But these new things will soon become old, and since you looked good only in those 'new things', so after some time there is an urge to find more new things and this vicious circle continues. All this starts from feeling low or bad about yourself, which further brings many different feelings and emotions that takc away happiness from you. It leads to an inferiority complex, fear, greed, resentment, arrogance and many such feelings which are not good for your happy life. No good decision can be made when you are surrounded by difficult emotions. You feel that if you have a big car only then will you be accepted in the society you live in; travelling internationally only suits "your kind of profile"; if your children are not studying in that "high end school" then what will your colleagues think of you and so on.

If you don't realise that you are trying to satiate feelings with material things then actually you are further aggravating the problem. And all these kinds of feelings impact your spending behaviour and you become used to spending high. This is a very common problem I have seen in many families, where the person says that I am earning well, spending modestly, but still do not generate enough investible surplus. "Itna kamane ke baad bhi kuch nahi bachta."

The problem is somewhere else and you keep blaming your employer for less salary and cursing the government for high inflation and taxes.

Budgeting sounds like a dangerous word. It's like dieting, where you need to restrict yourself to a specific diet and avoid specific foods. It's like restricting yourself from fun, but in the pursuit of some long-term goal.

In my experience restrictions do not work. It increases your craving, and you tend to eat (read spend) more. You have to have a very strong will power if you really want to follow a diet or a budget. But it is also true that both budget and diet have a common purpose i.e. keeping you healthy. You have to understand this before getting signs of diabetes, blood pressure or many such lifestyle diseases, and similar issues in your money matters.

So, first things first, you have to accept that it is important. You need to be aware that something is wrong with you which needs to be worked on, else it may trouble you in the future.

The key to less spending is awareness.

To understand the overall cash flow situation and to find out the root cause of the problem one needs to be watchful and cautious about money flow. You may not accept or sometimes may not be aware of having some behavioural issue with the money, but being mindful to your money flow will show you the real picture of your own self.

In the above 3 stories, you can see that if they were aware of their behaviour and were in sync with their purpose, they would have known the impact of their decisions on their finances. With this knowledge, they would not have done what they did or at least restricted themselves from overspending and focused on their life goals.

One should be aware of the larger purpose in life. I have heard people saying that we earn to eat. That's fine, but what we eat is our choice. We don't earn to eat only junk food. In the same way many people say that they earn to spend, and this is their money they can do whatever they want to. That's again fine, as I said earlier that first you need to accept that there is a problem and be ready to work on it. Staying healthy requires proactive effort; else you will always see yourself recovering from sickness.

Let me give you a simple exercise here.

Start noting down each and every penny that goes out of your system. Either you are paying in cash or through net banking, credit cards, auto debits, cheques or card swipes. Everything needs to be noted down. Even if you are going to get it back as reimbursement from your employer, or you are buying something for your parents or you are donating money to someone, you should have a record of every penny.

Keep your emotions out of the exercise. Remember this is just an accounting exercise and you just have to note down the numbers. Do not come to any conclusion at this point. No blame, no shame. Involve your family members in this. If your spouse has his/ her own income, then let her do the same exercise separately. If you have some joint expenses, then do write each your share separately in your own list of expenses. For now, just be yourself, do not start judging anything.

This is not just accounting; this is a process of self-discovery. This is just another way to show money that you are responsible towards it, that you are being good towards it. The money, for which you have spent considerable life energy to earn, is just asking for attention from you. It is another way of being considerate towards your effort. After all what we are doing is for a larger purpose and when the purpose is large, then it will demand your time and attention.

Use pocket diaries, mobile phone apps, small paper, whatever you feel comfortable with, but do remember to collate the data at one place every day. To start with, you may find some difficulty as recording data is not your habit. Arrogance may crop in and you may start saying that this is your money, you can do whatever you would like to do, why should you keep records? You may get emotional while entering the amount that you spent on the candies you bought for your child, or gifts bought for your parents and try to ignore that amount completely. Or you may even think of noting down only the bigger expenses, and ignore the smaller ones.

But remember, every penny matters. As the popular quote by Benjamin Graham goes **"Beware of the little expenses, a small leak will sink a great ship."** And remember that by noting down your expenses you are showing respect towards your money, that you know where have you spent it. You have not misplaced the same.

Don't just record your expenses, but also your income. Just like you need to account for all the expenses, even the smallest ones. We always tend to record the big entries and ignore the small ones, but do note that smaller ones are equally useful. So do not just note your monthly salary income, but also rental income, the dividend earned, interest income, gifts etc. Every penny has its value. The idea is to be aware of where the money is going and coming from.

After a few months of this honest accounting exercise when you know the actual flow of money, then starts the actual awareness exercise. Finding out the WHY part of your spending.

Look deep into your expenses and try to further divide the same into different sub heads to find out the reason you have spent that money. Your outflow could be your need, want or desire. What's the story behind that spending? What did you actually spend? Was it only money or time and health also?

This is the moment of truth, when you answer yourself. Keep in mind that there's nothing to be ashamed of anything. Notice the emotion behind your spending. Was it driven by an actual need, or was there some emotion behind it? The more aware you are about your cash flow, the more sensitive you will become towards your needs and follow a structured process to be in control. You will find out the leaks in the ship. You will get to know which area can be managed well to reduce more on expenses and time.

Generally, it is the discretionary expenses where you will find the leak. The money which is spent thoughtlessly or calling as one-time expenses on "sale" or under the emotions subhead "like to look good", to replace the old with new even if the old is working fine, to buy new gadgets which are not to be used at all.

Monthly expenses			
Items	**Monthly Amount (Self)**	**Monthly Amount (Spouse)**	**Monthly amount (Total)**
A. Housing			
Rent + Society Charges			
House Repairs			
Total Housing expenses			
B. Utilities			
Electricity			
Gas			
Water			
Telephone			
Mobile Phone			
Internet			
Cable TV			

Total Utilities expenses			
C. Food, Clothing, Transport			
Fruit/Vegetable/ Groceries			
Takeaway Food/ Restaurants			
Clothing			
Petrol			
Vehicle Maintenance			
Vehicle Taxes/License			
Driver Salary			
Servant Salary			
Others (Parking, Tolls, Bus, Taxi)			
Total Food, Clothing, Transport Expenses			
D. Education			
School Fees			
Tutoring/Books			
Sports/Out of School Activities			
School Bus/Transport			
Total Education Expenses			
E. Other Expenses			
Medical Cost			
Personal Care (Hair Care, Dry Cleaning Etc)			
Dependent Care			
Entertainment			

Recreation			
Hobbies			
Gift/Donation to Charities			
Gift to Family and Others			
Subscriptions (Newspapers and Magazines)			
Pocket Money-Children			
Wine/Spirits/Alcohol			
Cigarette/Tobacco			
Gardening Expenses			
Servants			
Drivers			
Total Other Expenses			
Total Expenses (A+B+C+D+E)			

Items	Day 1	Day 2	Day 3	Day 4	Day 5	Day 6	Day 7... and So On
A. Housing							
Rent							
House Repairs							
B. Utilities							
Electricity							
Gas							
Water							
Telephone							
Mobile Phone							

Internet							
Cable TV							
C. Food, Clothing, Transport							
Fruit/ Vegetable/ Groceries							
Takeaway Food/ Restaurants							
Clothing							
Petrol							
Vehicle Maintenance							
Vehicle Taxes/ License							
Driver Salary							
Servant Salary							
Others (Parking, Tolls, Bus, Taxi)							
D. Education							
School Fees							
Tutoring/ Books							
Sports/Out of School Activities							
School Bus/ Transport							
E. Other Expenses							
Medical Cost							

Personal Care (Hair Care, Dry Cleaning Etc)							
Dependent care							
Entertainment							
Recreation							
Hobbies							
Gift/Donation to Charities							
Gift to Family and Others							
Subscriptions (Newspapers and Magazines)							
Pocket Money-Children							
Wine/Spirits/ Alcohol							
Cigarette/ Tobacco							
Gardening Expenses							
Servants							
Drivers							
Total Expenses (A+B+C+D+E)							

CASH FLOW ANALYSIS

	Jan	Feb	Mar	Apr	May	Jun	Jul	Aug	Sep	Oct	Nov	Dec	Year
Income													
Salary (Post tax)													
Reimbursements													
Others (LTA/ Medical)													
Interest/dividends													
Rental Income													
Miscelleneous													
Total Inflow													
EXPENSES													
Home													
Mortgage/rent													
Home repaires													
Electricity													
Gas													
Water													

Telephone													
Mobile Phone													
Cable TV													
Interent													
Others													
Home Totals													
Daily living													
Fruit/Veg/ Groceries													
Dining out													
Clothing													
Petrol													
Vehicle Maintenance													
vehicl Taxes													
Driver Salary													
Servent Salary													
Others													
Daily living totals													

Child care Expenses													
School Fees													
Books/Tutorials													
Sports/Out of school Activities													
School Bus Transport/Boaring Expenses													
Pockt Money													
Others													
Transportation totals													
Others													
Mediacl Cost													
Personal care													
Dependent Care													

Entertainment													
Recreation													
Hobbies													
Donation/ Charities													
Gift to Family													
Subscriptions (Newspaper/ Magazine)													
Wine/Spirit/ Alcohal													
Cigarette/Tobacco													
Gardening													
Others													
Total													

Your spending structure will tell you your lifestyle, your discretionary and fixed expenses, what are your basic needs and what you spend for fun. What expenses you cannot compromise on and what you can try to reduce so you can have more surplus to save more, so you can spend more on what's required. It's all about spending. Yes. You save now to spend in the future. But if you spend now and if you have a future too, what will you do then?

Let me tell you my story here. Last February when I did this budgeting exercise, I had many revelations. I do this every year, so I am also of the opinion that I know where my money is going. Normally I do it every August, but this time I did this in February too, as I shifted to a new place and I could sense that something had happened in my expenses account, which I should work on. As my wife manages this budgeting department, I took her help and sat along with her, carrying my credit card and bank statements. We found that our telephone and internet expenses had shot up by almost 66%. What used to be around Rs 3,000 p.m. was now Rs 5,000 p.m., there were 2 magazines and 1 additional newspaper that I recently subscribed to, which increased my monthly billing by Rs 200. And due to our move, our eating out also increased. I immediately called up customer care and got my mobile plan tweaked, so as to come back to my old amount or at least lesser than the current one. I also called the newspaper vendor and told her to cancel my magazine subscriptions as I read articles online. Now you must be thinking that these are peanuts, and why should I be worried about this cost and how does this impact overall finances? See, these are my finances, and I track it every six months and take necessary steps to reduce it.

In yours the figures may be different and this Rs 2,200 per month, could be Rs 10-20k per month. I value my Rs 2,200 as this turns out to be Rs 26,400 p.a., which is somewhere near to what my financial planner charges, this also equals my annual life insurance premiums; if I save this amount then I may be able to save more for my foreign vacation, this Rs 2,200 per month may add Rs 20 lakh more in my retirement kitty and so on.

Do you see? The different ways I can use my savings would not have been possible if I was not aware of my outflows and or done a budgeting exercise. Carl Richards in his book One-Page Financial Plan, says that many of us view budgeting as a punishment, a way to hold ourselves back from buying the things we want, a way to feel guilty about paying for the things we need; but actually budgeting is not about numbers, it's about awareness. Its purpose is not to punish ourselves for spending money; it's to become very aware of how we are spending our money so that we have enough for the things that matter most.

You don't know where your money is going, unless you track it. Your spending structure gives you the opportunity to see the gap between what you say is important and how you spend your money. For example, if you like travelling the most and this is even in your goal sheet that you are a travel freak, yet you spend a major portion of money on clothes. Or you say that you are a big foodie and love tasting a variety of food by visiting different places, but your spending structure shows that you spend your money on gadgets (phones and tablets).

However, it is also true that sometimes life happens. Your car breaks down, or you meet with an accident, your phone suddenly stops working or you have to replace your home sofas, some urgent home repairs etc. but all these are truly one-time events or sometimes emergencies. The problem would come when one-time events become regular ones, like when you keep shopping online on every sale announced, by justifying "for this time only...this is a good deal".

You can make adequate provisions for emergencies and even for your annual shopping, but when you use these "sales and promotions" as your one-time event excuse, then you are actually throwing planning out of window. Please understand that besides these online shopping sprees, there are many "one-time events" you will experience like when you need a special treat; "no cooking Wednesdays"; when India wins or when India loses (in sports); when you are fed up of work and want to go on a weekend break; birthday parties of your spouse, kids, friends, relatives, kid's friends; or festivals. Through budgeting we try to plug the gaps, so our hard-earned money should be used and invested the way we actually want it to be used. Carl Richards says that budgeting is important not only because it reminds us not to spend so much on eating out or fuel, but also because it helps us cultivate the awareness we need to save and spend in accordance with our values.

Budgeting is Boring

You must be thinking that budgeting sounds like a boring job? Yes. I completely agree with you. It's quite difficult to dig deeper into expenses to figure out your complete cash outflow, and that too just to find out if your spending structure is good for your financial future or you have to cut down on that. Moreover, cutting down on spending itself is a very depressing thing. Sometimes personal cash flow analysis is also embarrassing for those who think that they are careful in spending, and doing this exercise may reveal many uncomfortable things.

This is why the easier thing is to avoid getting into this exercise and just focus on the investments as in where to invest and when to invest. The word financial planning itself sounds very boring, but investing is exciting. A general sense is that when the path to achieve goals is only through investments, then why get into such spending details. Well, this is where you ignore the rules of the game.

Cash flow is the blood line of any financial process; if this is not in order your complete life can be in the doldrums. Can your employer pay you a regular salary if the company's cash flows are not being managed properly? You must be aware of what happened with Kingfisher Airlines. They were highly in debt and revenues were slowly coming down. Unnecessary spending was on the rise, and when banks stopped restructuring loans, the bomb exploded.

The same could happen in personal finance if you can't control your personal cash flows. It's not only about creating and following a budget, but also understanding the pattern of spending, sources of income and the areas to improve on. Understanding your personal cash flow helps in goal setting, it prepares you for uncertain times. Let me explain how.

Let's understand it with retirement planning. Retirement planning is about managing your current finances and investing the surplus generated in such a way that you can accumulate a decent amount, that ensures comfortable post-retirement years when you will not be getting a monthly income. The corpus should be enough to generate you the income required to manage your then lifestyle. And at that time, your savings will be your only source of income generation. Now, do you think that just giving a numerical figure to this goal justifies the planning process?

Of course, not.

Your monthly/annual basic plus lifestyle spending will lead to one figure to achieve, but staying intact with the same figure, also needs a regular cash flow review.

In fact, regular cash flow reviews are important post retirement also, to keep within your spending limits. To save towards your goals, you need to have enough money available with you for investments and for that too, cash flow understanding is must. If there's not enough money then either you have to rework on your goals or generate enough surplus by following a budgeting technique, and both involve personal cash flow understanding.

This is not all. On the way to retirement you will meet so many other goals, desires/wishes and unexpected expenses like annual vacations, children education & marriage, buying new house, changing car every 4-5 years, house repairs, house furniture replacement, medical emergencies, close relative marriage etc. To achieve your long-term goals, you need to manage your day-to-day spending structure to stay planned for most of the things. Making a big-ticket purchase may also require taking loans, and managing those repayments require understanding and comfort with the cash flow situation. Although banks will look at it from the angle of the borrower's repayment capacity, financial planning will also look on the impact it will bring on other goals. Debt management and goal planning go hand in hand.

Insurance planning also depends on cash flow analysis. A proper back up plan is as important as a sound and stable investment plan. You may have a number of insurance policies in your portfolio, but if you are not sure of the adequacy of insurance cover then you are just wasting your time and money. Your total life insurance cover should be enough to protect your financial responsibilities and future goals, in your absence. Here again your cash flow analysis will play its part, as to find out adequate insurance cover, you need to have a clear idea on the spending pattern, loans taken and goals targeted.

Lipid Profile Check Through Cash Flow Analysis

Besides goals or purchases, you may consider cash flow analysis as a lipid profile check of your cash flows. A lipid profile is the blood screening test which is done to check your heart health. The function of the heart is to supply blood, oxygen and other nutrients to other body parts through the circulatory system, and if the blood carries a high quantity of fats, then it will impact the functioning of the heart. If the level of fats is too high then it starts accumulating in the arteries which are the main cause of cardiovascular issues. No, I am not going to tell you how to keep your heart healthy by keeping your lipid profile in check, but I am just relating the lipid profile with basic financial health check ratios which everyone should do on a regular basis to keep their finances healthy.

Cash flow is the bloodline of the personal financial profile and keeping it healthy should be the first and foremost concern in financial management. Let's relate financial health check ratios with lipid profile constituents to understand it better.

1. LDL Cholesterol and Bad EMIs

LDL is Low-Density Lipoprotein, considered to be bad cholesterol as it contributes to the fatty build up in the arteries. So high levels of LDL are not at all good for health. Similarly, bad EMIs, like personal loans, credit card dues/loans, sometimes even car loans are not good for your financial health. Although loans in any form is not ideal, still something which is used towards consumption and not production is considered to be very bad. Bad EMIs increase the burden on cash flow, and also do not participate in any asset building. These are a pure waste of important resources, which otherwise could be used towards building up productive assets or increasing earnings. Your total EMIs should not exceed 40% of your monthly income and if it is only for bad loans then the percentage should be 10-15%.

2. HDL Cholesterol and Savings

The role of HDL (High-Density Lipoprotein) is to carry LDL cholesterol away from the arteries and back to the liver. There it's broken down and passed through the body. Some part of LDL gets cleansed with the help of HDL. So, a healthy level of HDL is required in the blood. So are your savings. Where the savings could help you achieve your long and short-term goals, there it also helps in curbing the urge to take non-productive loans and thus manage the bad EMIs level well. Savings should start from the day you get your first pay check and should at least be 20% of your monthly income, even if you are not targeting any goals.

3. Triglycerides and Total Debt to Asset ratio

Triglycerides are the form in which most fat exists in the body. High levels of triglycerides, with low HDL and high LDL, increase the risk of coronary artery disease. In personal finance, you may treat the high debt levels i.e. total liabilities, unsuitable insurance policies or other financial products as a metaphor for triglycerides. High debt levels in combination with low savings and high bad EMIs, increase the risk of financial disaster. Ideally, your total debt value should not be more than 50% of your assets.

A ***lipid profile*** is one of the many medical tests conducted to check the overall health of the person. Same way debt and cash flow analysis is one of the many areas which needs to be watched for overall financial health.

You need to keep your risk profile (blood pressure) in check while making investments. You have to have a proper asset allocation (balanced diet) suitable to your risk profile and goals, so the required nutrients and that too in adequate quantity should be given to the body (personal finances). When your personal cash flow is positive and you can afford to build a surplus, then you can have an emergency fund to fall back on in case of an unexpected event. You will be in a position to pay in cash for your purchases instead of swiping credit cards and rolling it over. And also, you would be in a position to seriously work towards your financial goals.

But on the other side, if you are cash flow negative then I don't think any of your investments towards your goals can stay intact. You will run after returns and look out for ways to make more money in a short period of time. Following a process would be next to impossible as you may require money at any point of time.

The bottom line is that personal cash flow management is an integral part of financial planning. Getting hold of your personal cash flow is like half the battle won for a better financial future.

RISK IS BEYOND THE KNOWN

Risk is Beyond the Known

99% of business ideas don't see the light of day because of only this worry. Every third person wants to be an entrepreneur but continues with their jobs for only one reason. I did not appear for CAT and settled for a Regional Management Exam with this doubt in mind. My mother in law does not let her grandson ride a bicycle on the road because of this fear. Sahil never proposed to Ritika because of this hesitation. Many investors prefer to only watch the markets and do not invest in because of this.

Do you know what "this" is?

The fear of failure. The risk, as you might have called it, if you understand it that way.

People do not even give it a try with this doubt in mind, **which sometimes is the main reason towards their despair, distress, disappointment.**

But one has to understand that there is the other side of the coin too.

The business idea could have become the next Flipkart, Ola or Paytm. You may succeed in your own venture or you may start loving your job after trying this new thing. Clearing CAT may not be that difficult as it seemed in the first place. Ritika could have said yes, and participating in the equity markets might have supported you in wealth generation or at least made you a wise investor.

So, it may not be wise to call it as only failure. It is just that you perceived it as a failure, but the outcome was not known upfront.

Risk is an unknown territory. It is a chance, a probability. This is the reason you never have a clear answer as to what to do. It always has 2 sides to it. It's not YES or NO. It's in between as in MAY BE or could be BOTH. If you can tell with certainty that failure is guaranteed then why would you do that, and if you are sure of the success then why wouldn't you?

Wikipedia says that risk is the potential of gaining or losing something of value. Values (such as physical health, social status, emotional well-being, or financial wealth) can be gained or lost when taking risk resulting from a given action or inaction, foreseen or unforeseen (planned or not planned).

If you look at the positive side of it, you may call risk as opportunity, where as some may call it a threat. Both are correct. But whatever you think, it is not possible to accept only one side of it. **Not acting itself is a risk.**

You may act upon a thing perceiving the positive side of it, but the outcome could be the other way around. Same way not acting on something perceiving only the negative side of it, where the results could have been positive. This is how life goes.

Action in this unknown territory depends on 3 important factors:

1. Risk Capacity
2. Risk Required
3. Risk Tolerance

Winning is what everyone wants but what if you lose? Understanding the quantum of damage it may bring in your life and how much that would impact your life is what that determines your risk capacity. For example, a student has a good risk capacity for doing hit and trial with his career options. Age is on his side; if he loses the competition, he has multiple attempts available to retry.

Where as a parent may not have that much money saved to let the child keep trying with options. They may prefer that he get into some architecture or BSc kind of option as an alternative to engineering. The money in hand and active work life available to them may define the risk capacity. But here the question is of a child's future and one may not like to put pressure on him. Moreover, it's always advisable to give child a free hand with good counselling and guidance so that he may go with a good career choice. This means it's worth taking the risk and risk is required in this case.

However, parents are already catering to home loans, car loans, and the job scenario is also looking bleak.

Moreover, they are also not confident on the child's ability to come out with flying colours. So, if after investing so much they do not get returns as expected it would be a great disappointment and stress for them. Thus, they are still reluctant in funding further tries. This shows the risk tolerance.

In the above-mentioned case, you may see that the parents have lower risk capacity and risk tolerance, however the risk required is high. The understanding of the risk helps you better manage it and accept it up to your maximum tolerance, but it does not help you control the outcomes. In other words, it helps you live your life well. It helps you keep looking forward and progressing. It does not let you live in fear always. But only if it is taken up to a tolerable level.

Understanding risk always leads you take calculated actions. Like if you always remain afraid of failure you would never be able to start the business (if at all you want to); volatility in markets will never let you invest; competition in the market will never let you strive. But only when you accept the outcome in any form, and plan for all "what if" scenarios then only you would be able to understand the best case and worst-case scenarios.

In money transactions, risk is very commonly discussed and viewed upon. So, after knowing your net worth situation, your cash flow position, your goals and responsibilities as discussed in the previous chapters and before approaching a financial planner or doing it yourself, you should better have a clear understanding on what risk is all about.

Let's understand RISK better.

- Does the word risk haunt you or excite you?
- Do you consider risk as an opportunity or uncertainty?
- Do you agree that even so-called safe investments are risky?
- What is riskier – investing or not investing?
- Which has more risk – equity or real estate?
- Is financial planning risky or the risk is in not doing planning at all?

Answers to the above questions depend on your understanding of the word risk and types of risks. Generally, the word risk is taken the same as loss, but actually, it's not so. There are so many definitions of risks. Everything around you has some sort of risk factor in it. The medicines you take may cure you or give you some allergic reaction. The sport you play may injure you. The car you drive may break down. Some risks cannot be avoided, you either have to manage it or transfer it. If there is no option of management or transfer, then you have to accept it and prepare yourself for the consequences in such a way that the damage is less. This leads me to give a broad breakup to the ***types of risks*** when you are dealing in the investment market, and all these are known risks. But some among them are ignored.

> "Risk comes from not knowing what you are doing." - ***Warren Buffet***

So, when you know what you are doing, you are playing in the "known risk" categories. But the real risk lies in the unknown territory.

Types of Risks: Known Risks

They say financial markets are the reflection of the economy as a whole. If the economy is doing well then financial markets should also be performing well and vice versa. Now, this also means that anything specific happening in the economy (good or bad) is going to impact your overall investments as well (positively or negatively), and you can't do anything about it. This is what systemic risk is. **Systemic Risk** is something which impacts the whole economy, country, or a broader group and thus affects each and every constituent of the same. Inflation risk, market risk, political risk, interest rate risk, are some of the examples of systemic risk.

Un-systemic Risk, on the contrary, is a type of risk that impacts a particular section of the group – company, stock, security. Say for example, government raising taxes on tobacco will impact ITC in a major way, but not pharma, steel or cement companies. Tata and Infosys groups' internal issues will not impact any other company in their specific sector.

Inflation Risk – Rise in general prices impacts every company, household and even governments for that matter. High inflation results in high expenditure and also higher cost of production. The higher cost of production has a spiralling effect and further increases the prices of the final output. In a growing economy, you cannot save yourself from inflation risk. Moreover, a reasonable inflation rate is healthy for economic growth. Inflation is a slow poison. Its impact is not visible with the naked eye but in retrospect only. We all know the cost of things 10 years earlier; except for mobile recharges, I guess the price of everything has risen!

Market Risk – Market risk is a systemic risk which will impact each and every of its constituents. If market sentiments are weak, then all stocks, even if under good management and stable and growing businesses, will get affected. Recall 2008: each and every company in the stock market fell, although good companies recovered faster. For a short time, it impacted even the debt segment of the market.

Currency Risk – This type of risk is also called exchange rate risk. Just like stock markets, currency rates also get affected by many different factors. The movement in currency rates may impact your investments if you have directly invested in another country of your residence, just like NRIs do in India. This will also impact your domestic investments if the company you have invested in has international business and dealings. In today's kind of global economy, it is difficult to keep yourself safe from currency risk. However corporate houses do trade in currency derivatives to hedge such risk to have the least impact on their balance sheets and your investments.

Political Risk – Any country's policy-making depends solely on the political stability and situation. The government at the centre will play its shots which may or may not be taken positively by the market, citizens and corporates. This is not only about the political scenario in your own country, but also where your investments are, where your business dealings and operations are. Country-specific policies on immigrants and taxation will directly impact NRIs working there and also companies having operations there. India government policies directly impact Indians and also MNCs having operations here.

Taxation Risk – Inflation and taxes are considered to be two holes in the pocket. Both suck your money out of your system. High taxes directly impact your cash flow. High taxes mean lower profit after tax of the companies you have invested in. Though high taxes sometimes also mean improvement in governments' fiscal front, but from a personal and corporate finance point it is an outflow.

Interest Rate Risks – Interest rate scenario is being managed by RBI in India, through its monetary policies. Inflation and growth are the two major concerns which drive RBI decisions on interest rates.

In a high inflationary scenario, you will see interest rates going up, as RBI wants to control the supply of money to control inflation, and when growth concerns are high then the interest rates generally are on a downward trend. Interest rates impact your loans, business cost of capital, inflation and thus you.

Credit Risk – Also known as default risk. This type of risks impacts you when you have given a loan to someone or invested in debt instruments. Credit risk is the risk of not getting your capital back along with the timely interest pay-outs. It is the risk of the creditworthiness of the borrower. Would you lend to your friend who has been a known defaulter and has never returned money to other lenders? This is a credit risk.

Liquidity Risk – Liquidity generally signifies the quantum of cash flow in your profile or how easily your investments will be liquidated and in what time. Banks lend to you or your business looking at the liquidity position. Even if you have many properties in your name, but do not have a regular and stable earning source, banks will be reluctant to lend to you. Your expenses and goals will be met by paying money, not by just staying invested in some instruments even if they are growing. You need liquid money for your requirements.

Types of Risks – Some Known but Ignored Risks

Information Risk – These days you are bombarded

with so much information on almost all areas of finance which makes decision making actually very difficult. And the situation worsens when you start taking information as knowledge. You make financial decisions based on the case studies you read in business papers, Q&A on personal finance TV shows, or reading some advisors answering queries in a magazine or a website. You try to copy that advice as if the situation described in the question is exactly similar to yours. But this is not the right way, as every person's financial situation, needs, wants, goals, aspiration, attitude, is different.

Health Risk – We know that in today's kind of scenario, no one is immune to health problems. With age, we are prone to many illnesses. Also, due to our deteriorating lifestyle, we invite many diseases ourselves. Making and multiplying money is fine, but all this will be washed out if health is not taken care of well. This is known to every one of us, but hardly anyone is working on it.

Life Risk – Or I should call it a Death Risk? This can't be managed, everyone has to die someday, but at least by understanding this, we can make such arrangements so that our dependents do not suffer due to our mismanaged issues.

Longevity Risk – Though we are not sure, but with the improvement in medical facilities, our lifespan has been increasing. There is a treatment available for all major illnesses. We may live long, but with a deteriorating lifestyle, we are hitting the quality of life very badly. It's not only about health but money also. You can never be sure how much is enough. But you should try to have enough so that your savings last longer than you.

Behaviour Risk – We are a victim of our own behaviour, so our mood swings, behaviour biases, notions built on good and bad past experiences are a risk to our investments. In search of safe instruments, we tend to get into illiquid low-yielding insurance policies, we go overboard on a particular asset class in the lure of getting high returns and forget the diversification rules. We prefer having real estate as on one side it gives us a high, and also because we have seen our parents make money from this in the past. And in all this we forget the liquidity risk.

We think that whatever is happening currently or happened in the recent past is the only reality and the future will continue in the same manner. We believe that if everyone else is doing one thing then we should also do the same and this way we feel secure in our decisions. All this and much more are the reasons investors don't make money even when investments generate it. Because we keep investing and withdrawing from our investments, at the wrong time, with wrong reasons and this results in underperformance. One of the major behaviour risks/ anomalies is instant gratification. Basically, instant gratification is all about focusing on the immediate benefit, without realizing its impact on our life later. It is like preferring to kill the goose to get all the golden eggs in one go.

In investments too, this behaviour is very common among people. We want everything instantly and this can be proved with people's behaviour:

a) Avoiding insurance when you are fine and searching for the same when you are about to hospitalised, expecting it to take care of your expenses instantly.
b) Ignoring tax saving in April and running for investments in January when asked to submit investment proofs.
c) Acting on stock tips to make instant and fast returns, even after knowing that stocks are for the long term.
d) Investing for the long term but watching the performance on a daily basis, as it gives feeling of instant satisfaction if it is rising or disappointment if falling.

The types of risks I've listed are not exhaustive. As I said that there is some sort of risk in everything we do. These are just names given to understand the risks so we may take necessary precautions or arrangements to manage the same well. Once you understand and accept the risk, you will figure out the way to manage it. Some ways are defined and already structured like diversification, asset allocation and financial planning, and some get innovated in the process.

What is Risk Management?

You would be better able to manage the things you know well. Now when you know what types of risks may haunt you and bother in the process of portfolio designing or living a comfortable life, you may work out on how you would be able to better manage it. But those risks which are not known or are not visible to naked eye or even in past experiences, you can't do anything about them. But accept them. When I discuss risk management with my clients or in any seminar, the normal tendency is to assume it on the insurance aspects. But actually, it is a wide subject.

Insurance is no doubt one of the risk management tools where we transfer some of our risks to the insurance company. But there are a lot of other risks, which can't be transferred and have to be managed internally, through different other risk management tools like risk avoidance, risk optimisation, risk transfer and risk retention. Yes, your risk management revolves around these 4 aspects only. Let me give you a brief on this before discussing some personal finance situations.

1. **Risk Transfer:** This is the first and foremost solution to risk management. If possible, you should always transfer the risk inherent in your decision to a third party which normally comes in the form of an insurance company. The risk of managing high medical costs can be taken care to some extent by buying health insurance.

The death risk or providing to the future of the family in your absence can be transferred to a life insurance company by buying an adequate life insurance cover. Risks involved in businesses or loss due to fire, burglary, natural calamities may get easily transferred to general insurance company. If you can think about the risk, then the first step should be to find out if that can be transferred or not. If yes, then go for it and if not check out other strategies.

2. **Risk Avoidance:** When you know that the specific risks that you are going to take cannot be transferred then you may prefer to completely avoid that risk. In the words of Warren Buffet, "All I want to know where I am going to die, so I will never go there."

   Take the example of adventure sports. No life insurance company covers death while playing adventure sports so you may completely avoid playing adventure sports if you want to be safe and insured always. Similarly, no insurance company pays a claim due to abuse of drugs or alcohol, so you may completely avoid the risk by limiting your alcohol intake. If you do not want to take risk of default or credit risk as explained above, then you may completely avoid lending to a person or corporate or an investment having a low credit profile. But frankly in most cases, you just cannot avoid risks. You have to take a risk to move forward.

3. **Risk Optimisation:** The risks that cannot be transferred or avoided have to be seen from an optimisation angle. There are some risks which can be optimised well. Optimisation means to manage it in such a way so that its bad impact should bother you the least. But please keep in mind that once you are optimising the bad impact, the good impact also gets automatically optimised. For example, in financial investments, if you want to keep yourself safe from volatility, and prefer to stay in fixed income instruments, then on one side have the safe portfolio and security from market movements, but on the other side limit yourself from a good long-term growth.

   Two of the most popular risk optimisation techniques work well in investment management too. These are diversification and asset allocation. Some of the un-systemic risks can be managed quite well with the diversification technique.

   As per Investopedia, **diversification** is a risk management technique that mixes a wide variety of investments within a portfolio. The rationale behind this technique contends that a portfolio constructed of different kinds of investments will, on an average, yield higher returns and pose a lower risk than any individual investment found within the portfolio. Diversification strives to smooth out un-systemic risk events in a portfolio so that the positive performance of some investments neutralizes the negative performance of others. Therefore, the benefits of diversification hold only if the securities in the portfolio are not perfectly correlated. Currency risk can be managed by diversifying investments in different countries. Sector risk can be diversified by having investments in different sectors. Interest rate risk can be managed by diversifying into fixed rate and market-linked tradable debt securities, and so on.

The other strategy is asset allocation. This strategy calls you to divide your investments in different unrelated investment asset classes. The systemic risks like inflation risk, market risk etc. may be managed to some extent with this strategy.

We will discuss more on these strategies in the later sections.

4. **Risk Retention:** When there is no way out and still you have to take action then there is nothing you can do but retain the risk. For example, you cannot completely avoid the risk of accidents while driving. You may transfer the risk of personal and financial loss to the insurance company. You may optimise the risk by wearing a seat belt, driving a car with six air bags, getting your car well serviced on time, ensuring that tyres well inflated, but still you cannot control outer conditions and thus you have to retain the risk.

   Same goes with investments. You may invest in blue-chip companies and well-rated bonds, have proper diversification and allocation in place, have a financial plan in place with a well-documented strategy, and invest with discipline, but investment markets are governed by many other factors which is not in your control and you cannot fully manage the risk of market fall so you have to retain the risk.

Financial Planning as Risk management Tool

Anything that puts you into a process and builds your discipline is a risk management tool in itself. A process manages your behaviour risks and does not let you wander from your actions. Just imagine, how would you feel to put your child in a school where there is no syllabus, no classes, no timetable. You are told that everything can be customised as per their requirement or you may let your child study whatever he/she wants to. Complete freedom, no structure. Or how would you feel working in an office where there are no set HR guidelines, no role definition, no designed workflow, no processes or no obvious responsible authority.

We do not like chaos and surely do not want it in our lives too. And that is why a structure and process is a must in everything we work with. Be it academics, the work we do, the places we visit or the people we interact with. And when it comes to personal finance, the structure and discipline that is brought in by a strategic personal financial planning exercise. A structured approach considers your current financial health by understanding your cash flow, net worth, risk tolerance, the goals targeted and comes up with steps after considering all the risks coming from all the what-if scenarios like longevity risk, life risk, health risk, and puts you into a process to manage the information and behaviour risk.

Risk Tolerance Vs Risk Perception

In my practice when I ask my clients as to what kind of returns they want to see in their portfolio, the normal answer is that it should be in double digits. But when I further enquire on what percentage of portfolio fall they are comfortable seeing, they get defensive and reply in single digits. Of course, this is what we all would like to have. Low risk and high return. But unfortunately, this does not happen in the real world. You have to be open to risks when the expectations of returns are high. Also, you should not expect high returns if you want a conservative investments portfolio. Your comfort level with the kind of risk you are taking depicts **your risk tolerance**. In investment terminology it tells how much a person is willing for their portfolio to diminish for a chance to make bigger returns.

Sometimes an investor enters the stock market believing that his risk tolerance level is very high and is thus ready to bear the volatility. The same investor starts blaming the government, economy, inflation or may start calling equity investments as gambling in a market downturn. Why? because he misjudged his risk tolerance level. He enters with a perception in mind that he's young or having a good inflow of money or having very long-term goals etc. so he should be very high in equity allocation. But after a few months he finds that he cannot handle real volatility. It was all his perception which kept changing looking at the rising or falling market, reading media news, watching business channels or talking to inexperienced friends.

Risk perception is what you as an investor personally feel about your risk tolerance level. Buying more when markets are moving up and selling more when markets are going down is the result of your personal risk perception. According to research, bull and bear market phases barely change an investor's risk tolerance level, but what they change is the risk perception. Investors who do not follow a proper process in their investments often fall prey to their wrong decision making due to their own risk perception.

Why is risk profiling important before making investments?

Suffering losses due to underestimating the risk involved can be as disappointing as losing the opportunities to make investments on overestimating the potential risk involved. While making investments, it is as important to understand your reaction to different outcomes as it is to understand the probable outcomes. Risk profiling is just like a basic blood pressure check, to decide on how fast you can or should walk/run on a treadmill, when to slow and when to stop. **Risk profiling is the evaluation process to find out individual's willingness to take the risk.** This process defines the risk tolerance level of the investor after considering the understanding and acceptability of risk in different situations of life. However, unlike blood pressure, risk tolerance is quite difficult to gauge and it cannot be just a number to tell you how exactly you should devise your portfolio.

Like a doctor sometimes puts you on watch and takes time to set a suitable medicine for your health which suits your body type, in the same way sometimes advisors also take time to set your portfolio, by looking at your reaction to different market conditions. If you are a self-driven investor then it is very important for you to watch your behaviour with your portfolio and develop investment wisdom over time. The main reason of doing risk profiling is to figure out a suitable asset allocation as per your risk tolerance level. Once you know how much volatility you can handle then only you can decide what equity allocation you should have and in what funds.

What is the Risk in not doing Risk Profiling?

Well, on the face of it, there is no risk at all. After all this is just an awareness exercise which helps you meet you with yourself and know yourself better. If done in the right way, you get to know yourself much better. You will understand your preferences and your risk tolerance to have a better suited investment portfolio. If not done in the right way or not done at all and you invest with your perception which may be the result of many behaviour biases, built over time with your experiences or others' influence on you, you may under-allocate or over- allocate in a particular investment asset class. You may rebalance your portfolio only on the basis of market situations or it is also possible that you may not look at your portfolio in totality. You will just look at those areas which are getting impacted by market movements, and act with your limited understanding without having a structure in place.

Can You do Risk Profiling on Your Own?

There are many tools available to find out a person's risk tolerance. Some do it by asking 5-6 questions, and some do it through a detailed psychometric analysis. But whichever way one does it, there should always be a scope of discussion and reasoning to it. It should not only be something like how much risk you are going to take, how much you have taken in past, what is your age and profession because that will not lead to anywhere. For example, your acceptance of a job which offers salary as 50% fixed and 50% variable or habit of driving your vehicle above the speed limit surely depicts the way you look at the risk and may impact your risk tolerance in investments too, and thus may be a part of the overall discussion. Your understanding of risks also plays an important role in defining your risk tolerance. If you approach a financial planner or do it yourself, you need to be sure that you have taken inflation, interest rate and all such risks that we discussed above into consideration and have a well-accepted answer on the impact they will have on your financial plan and thus your financial life.

No Pain – No Gain / No Risk – No Success

> *"For one who see his life as a stepping stone towards a larger possibility, for him there is no fear of failure. For one who is looking at the simple events of life itself as the goals of life, for him there is abundance of success available."*
> - ***Sadhguru***

Life can never be smooth. This is what makes it exciting. The success can never be easy. This is what keeps us going. You need those moments which test you, to give you a learning or experience. If you stand by those with your head held high, you have gained wisdom. But if you keep yourself away from them under fear of failure you can never achieve success. Look into the eye of the risk or the fear you have, find out how you would be able to manage it well, else accept it and be friends with it. When you know that it is along with you, you will automatically take calculated steps.

ASSET ALLOCATION AND PERFECT INVESTMENT PORTFOLIO

Asset Allocation and Perfect Investment Portfolio

I have used the term Asset Allocation many times in the above sections. If you are new to personal finance management or used to investing only randomly then you might not be aware of this term. Actually, the overall purpose of doing risk profiling is to find out the suitable asset allocation, so it is important to understand what it actually means. In simple terms, asset allocation is dividing the investment amount among different unrelated investment asset classes with a goal of minimizing the volatility and optimizing returns with risks.

Unrelated assets mean those which do not respond to the same market forces in the same way at the same time. This may lead your investments to gain on one front when the other side is losing (however there may be instances when both are reacting the same way, but over a longer period of time this is how they should behave). It is just like having a balanced diet with a goal of taking all nutrients our body requires to stay healthy.

Asset allocation is a must to keep your investments healthy. An unseasoned investor may not like this approach, as where this strategy optimises the risk and return, there in a rising market scenario it may not deliver high returns. In other words, it optimises not maximizes. An inexperienced or novice investor gets attracted to the return and does not value the process, so with a lure of earning more returns she has a tendency to move into more of stock market investments, but this way there are high chances for her to burn her fingers.

The opposite is also true: in a volatile environment, investors tend to move towards safe assets, believing it will keep their investments safe, but what they do not realize is that inflation and taxation eat into their portfolio considerably. So, having a proper mix of different asset classes is what one requires.

Asset allocation represents the broad distribution of your investment, but within that allocation your asset location is also very important for achievement of goals. Asset location should be seen from the diversification point of view. It signifies the product where investment is made to gain exposure to particular asset class.

There are four main asset classes available in India for investments – equity, debt, gold and real estate. Within asset classes, there are multiple products available which can be selected based on near-, medium- and long-term requirements or goals. The main considerations while selecting a suitable product are risk, taxation and liquidity. Most of the risk portion gets managed at the asset allocation level; rest can be taken care of at the product level. Liquidity concerns clearly depend on the goal targeted and how the other aspects of financial planning like emergency funding, insurances etc. are being taken care of. The further along the goal, more of your investments can be locked in or invested in long-term products. Let's see the options available and how to select a particular product.

Equity

At the retail level you can have exposure in equity through three instruments – direct share purchase through stock market, equity mutual funds and Unit Linked Insurance Plans (ULIPs). While selecting the instrument you need to understand about the expertise required to manage the exposure, especially if you are going to invest on your own. Liquidity and taxation-wise, direct equity and equity mutual funds are the same. The difference lies in the professional management and diversification feature that mutual funds offer, of course with some costs attached. ULIPs also have professional management and diversification advantages, but being an insurance product, it has few other charges like mortality, allocation, administration etc. attached to it along with fund management charges. Also, the liquidity of the product is restricted, which may impact the rebalancing of asset allocation going forward.

Debt

There are multiple products available to get you the necessary exposure to this asset class. But while investing in this, along with the basic parameters of liquidity and taxation, one should also watch the interest rate scenario in the economy. In a falling interest rates scenario, the products with tradable securities give much better returns than the fixed ones. All bank products (savings, fixed deposit) and post office products (Public Provident Fund, National Savings Certificate, Senior Citizen Saving Scheme etc.) come under the debt category of investments, as do endowment insurance plans.

Even mutual funds offer debt exposure through diversified short-, medium- and long-term bonds. Corporate fixed deposits, non-convertible debentures, tax free bonds are all debt products. In simple terms when you receive a fixed interest from a product or the underlying product is a fixed income one it must be a debt structure, as debt is a synonym for loan. You take or you give, there is a fixed interest pay out in it.

Taxation-wise, most debt products generate taxable returns except PPF, endowment insurance plans (if it satisfies a few conditions) and tax-free bonds. Mutual funds fall under capital gain taxation which allows indexation of returns after three years. Indexation considerably reduces the amount of tax outgo. Post tax and inflation, returns of debt products are not very attractive. But still debt exposure is required in a portfolio to provide the necessary stability. It's always better to invest in non-taxable or low tax instruments, with a mix of fixed and tradeable products to bring the necessary push into debt instrument returns. Also do look at the cost structure of the product.

Gold

Indians don't require any asset allocation advice to buy gold. We are accustomed to buying gold on various occasions including weddings. This automatically gives us exposure to gold as an asset class. It is an important asset class that should be a part of every investment portfolio, but not more than 5%-10%. Few years back when the world economy was passing through a slowdown, we saw wonderful returns in gold. But the long-term return of gold is more or less equal to the inflation rate. That's why it is called as a "hedge against inflation". But it is not a suitable asset class for wealth generation.

Real estate

Real estate is the most popular asset class. Indians find safety in real estate. Even if we do not understand this asset in any sense, we feel pride in having one and assume that it never goes down in value. And due to the quantum of investment it asks for, many portfolios are skewed towards this particular asset class and thus compromise on the aspect of asset allocation. But you have to understand that this is the most illiquid asset class. You can't sell it with a click of a mouse. There's no ready market to sell this investment whenever required. One should be very careful while gaining exposure in real estate. You may have exposure to real estate by buying it in physical form or through Real Estate Investment Trusts (REITs). You should be very clear about the purpose of investment. Though having one's own house is fine it is not treated as an investment as it is for personal use. A second property should be bought with a clear goal in mind. This will help you decide whether to buy a residential or commercial property. Buying real estate most of the times involves a loan and thus impacts your cash flow too. So, it's always advisable to achieve your goals through liquid investments and get into real estate only when the cash flow permits.

A proper asset allocation with good fit products will give you a healthy portfolio and a real chance at achieving your goals.

Concept or Misconception of Perfect Investment Portfolio

When Sachin visited my office to discuss his investments, he specifically said that he was looking for a perfect investment portfolio. His current asset allocation was 70:30 (equity: debt) as suggested by one mutual fund advisor, but Sachin did not sound happy with it. He wanted to invest 100% in equity, with the reason that he doesn't require money for next 10 years. To top it up he was looking quite discontent with his existing investments, as his banker-suggested portfolio was showing higher growth than his existing portfolio.

So, what do you expect from me, I asked? I want you to have a look at my portfolio and suggest necessary changes, he replied. But your bank relationship manager has already pointed out the changes and moreover, you also want 100% exposure to equity then why do you want me to interfere in your investment portfolio?

Because somewhere I read that one should be more into equity when goals are far and this is what I want, but want to substantiate my belief from a financial planner, who can also tell me, looking at the current market scenario that have I lost the opportunity or is there still some juice left? Sachin added. It was 2017, and the recent stock market upsurge had brought back many such investors who wanted to take benefit of this rising scenario but were afraid of losing money too. Such kinds of investors usually make the mistake of investing heavily with wrong expectations and at the wrong time. And this category gets easily mis-sold with unsuitable products.

I handed over a risk profiling questionnaire to Sachin to answer. Looking at his responses to the questions I told him that had he approached me last year, I would have advised asset allocation of 50% growth and 50% defensive, way less than what he currently has. One who's bothered by a 20% fall in the market could not handle 100% equity portfolio.

Generally, people perceive a ***perfect investment portfolio*** as the one which generates maximum returns and at the same time expect it to fall the least in case of a downturn, which is not possible.

"There is no such thing as a perfect portfolio. We'll only know what was perfect in retrospect. There is, however, a portfolio strategy that will meet your needs. It's conceived from your financial situation, your understanding of risk, your time horizon and your desires."

– Rick Ferri

One "so called" perfect investment portfolio can be imperfect for another. The equity market does generate good returns in the long term, but it brings along volatility too. You should not get carried away by short term performance. This does not even mean that you should always invest safe. It's all about taking calculated risks keeping in mind your goals and risk tolerance.

A perfect investment portfolio should have the following features:

1. **Understandable:** First and foremost, a perfect investment portfolio is the one which is simple to understand. If you don't understand how your portfolio products work then how do you know they are perfect?

   Excuses like, some relative sold it to me or It helped my friend achieve his target or some stock expert was telling about this on CNBC or Manikaran reviewed this in his blog may not work in your favour. This is your money; you should know where you are putting it into.

2. **Manageable and flexible:** An investment portfolio which is flexible and easily manageable is a perfect portfolio. Flexible enough to come out and get in at any time, moving within products and asset classes should be easy. You should see your complete portfolio on a single page; it should not be scattered in different products exposed to the same asset class. You should be able to tell the current value of the portfolio within minutes. A perfect investment portfolio should give you peaceful sleep.

3. **Reasoning:** If you have a reason attached to every product you have invested in or in other words if there's a specific goal mapped to each product then that investment portfolio is perfect for you. Along with an understanding of the working of products you need to understand what role it plays in your total portfolio.

4. **Diversified and properly allocated:** Your portfolio should be allocated in various asset classes like equity, debt, gold, real estate etc. as per your risk tolerance level and goals targeted. It should be properly diversified within different sectors, countries, short- and long-term securities etc. A portfolio which is not meant to chase returns but follows a process to achieve goals is a perfect investment portfolio.

5. **Tax and cost efficient:** A perfect investment portfolio is the one whose returns don't get eaten up much by taxes or unnecessary costs attached to it. In other terms, while investing in any product you should be aware of the costs attached to it and taxability of returns. Insurance endowment plans do provide tax free returns but at the cost of total returns and this is due to a heavy inbuilt undisclosed expenses and investment structure.

   In the same way, real estate has different costs attached to it and also the returns are taxable. Having too much real estate and investment-linked insurance products are not good for your investment portfolio.

Searching for a perfect investment portfolio based on returns leads only to disappointment. "Perfect" or "All weather portfolios" are not real. No one can predict the future. Performance of different asset classes depends on many economic and political factors which is not possible for anyone to foresee. Even your financial planner cannot help you in that. His job is to design a proper process and strategy for your finances to make you a disciplined investor. Investing strictly on the basis of recent or past performance may result in a terrible portfolio which is not good for your financial health. The real perfect investment portfolio should help to plug in the behaviour gaps that come into play in different market scenarios. It should be the result of a properly laid down process that makes you stick to your investment plan without completely abandoning your strategy at the worst possible times.

This is the end of Section 2: Learning. Now you are better prepared and positioned to ask the right questions to your Financial Planner. You have learned what is important for you and your finances. It's not only about money, but also about time and health too. You have learned that emotional subjects get managed well if they are outsourced to professionals. Not because you cannot do it on your own, but because you are also emotional.

Now when you know what is important, why it is important, what needs to be tracked and taken control of, and why that needs to be tracked, then is time to understand more about YOU. As it is you who are responsible towards yourself and your surroundings. You are the one who can make or break your and many others' future.

So before approaching any financial planner, lets understand more about you.

Section 3
UNDERSTANDING

YOU ARE UNIQUE - DON'T FALL FOR SOCIAL PROOF

You are Unique - Don't Fall for Social Proof

I am sure that the exercises you did and learnings you had in the previous chapters must have revealed many things to you. It may have been quite distressing or exciting, depending on what you saw and interpreted out of it. It is natural to get emotional in gratitude, after realizing that there are many things in life you were not appreciating or have forgotten to value in the run of life, and similarly emotions may turn up when looking at your financial net worth.

You may have started appreciating your worth or may conclude that till this moment you were living in some fairy tale world and now have to do a lot of work on your responsibilities and achieve your goals. You must be going through many emotions if you have done your exercises seriously and gave a thought to your own story, your life journey. After all that was the moment of truth. But it's never wise to act, decide or plan when you are sailing in emotions. So, before moving forward, this is the time to pause.

Take your focus to your inner self, the silence within you. Take your attention away from the data. Pauses matter a lot in life. It gives you time to reflect. Just like in great music, it gives the listener and musician both a chance to breathe. It lets you to anticipate what might come next, and to appreciate what came before. A pause makes you look inside. It gives you time to review what you are doing and what you actually want to do. In this fast-paced world, you generally decide on the basis of what others are doing, or what others want you to do. But true happiness lies in knowing what you want to do. The mantra to have a happy and prosperous life is to recognize the important elements in your life and then work on them one by one. And to identify those elements – practice pause.

Pausing is a way of moving oneself away from the noise around. Just like you pause your TV when you receive a phone call to hear the other side clearly, the same way you need to pause the outer environment to hear your own self and also to your loved ones. It is about giving complete attention to the things you are doing or the person you are talking to, which may be your own self. Talking to your spouse or playing with children with a switched off phone and TV, is also another kind of pause. Reading a book with complete attention is a pause. Tasting and relishing food bite by bite is a pause. Listening to songs word by word is a pause. Appreciating nature is a pause.

You may call it mindfulness too. As per the Oxford dictionary mindfulness is a mental state achieved by focusing one's awareness on the present moment, while calmly acknowledging and accepting one's feelings, thoughts, and bodily sensations, used as a therapeutic technique. There is another variation of this saying, like "Be present in the moment" or "Live the moment" etc. All mean the same.

It may sound simple and easy, but do remember that doing simple things is the most difficult. Swami Vivekananda states that our mind does not stay fixed at one point. Like a monkey, it keeps jumping from one thought to another. Even Buddhism states that our mind cannot stay fixed on one thing for even 12 seconds. Do not confuse pausing with stillness. You don't have to be in a meditative state or concentrate on your breathing. It's just moving yourself away for a while from the noise and activities around. This is done to regain attentiveness, to revive relationships, to work on something more important in life, when you need more time for self or when you are rushing when you are not ready. Pausing before making a decision is a very helpful way of deciding right.

In finances too, I always recommend pausing for few minutes before spending (swiping cards). It's better to pause for few minutes or if possible, for 2-3 days before making any purchase. If the purchase is really important, you will come back to buy, else you have saved the money.

Practice pausing before investing. Think about why you want to invest, what for, why in this product. You should have all the acceptable reasons to do whatever you are doing. You need not justify your decisions to someone else but to your own self. Prosperity does not come from having more but enjoying more of whatever you have in your life. You can never be prosperous if you keep either bragging about your wealth or feel bad about what you have. You should respect your money, your family, your friends the way they are.

A pause will help you hear what Kiran Telang has very beautifully explained in her book Mindful Retirement, a concept called “Sound of Silence”. She says, this is the sound that most of us fail to hear in our lives. We are so surrounded by words and worldly noise that there is no silence within and outside. There is cacophony within us, our conversation with our own self never ceases, and with so much conversation happening we fail to hear the Sound of Silence. And if we do not have silence, how will we listen to our sub-conscious mind, which has all the answers that we seek, through words?

The pause will not result in anything immediately, but practicing to pause regularly will help you see yourself clearly. This will help you meet with the real YOU. What you do, why you do, for whom you do, who is that to you, why is the person or thing important in your life, what else can you do to improve upon your relationship with that person and are you doing that or not? How can you do that, do you really want to do that, what will it take to do the same, how prepared are you to do the same, can you do it on your own, should you do it on your own, what benefit will it bring you if you do it on your own, do you have something more important than this? There are so many more questions you will find the answer to when you regularly practice pause. To get the right answers you need to ask the right questions.

Knowing your own self is very important before you know others.

Let me tell you a story:

Saurabh, who is in his late 40s, and a doctor by profession approached me for his investments. He said he wanted to make the most of his money and thus preferred to invest where he could get the maximum return.

Saurabh was quite successful in his specific field and earned decently. He was new to the financial market. Till now he had invested or I should say accumulated only real estate and gold. He had some traditional investments too like PPF & bank FDs but was not exposed to stock markets yet. I sincerely had no answer to his question, as I actually did not know which product can get him "maximum return". Rather than just plainly saying no, I tried to dig deeper and asked him on his life and his professional journey and how did he manage to reach where he is right now. The idea was to know why did "maximum return" matter to him so much.

Since I asked him about his success story, I could sense the pride he felt in telling me the same. He told me that he completed his Post Graduation in 1994, and then joined a government hospital for a minuscule salary, but enough to take care of his basic needs. After 6 years of government service he left the job and started off with his own clinic by taking a bank loan on the clinic equipment. Since he had a good reputation among his patients, he did not encounter much trouble in setting up the practice and within a few years, he could clear off his debt completely.

After clearing his professional loan, he decided not to continue his clinic in the rented premises and bought his own commercial space, the first ever investment in his life. At that time, it was visibly a difficult decision financially but he took that risk. Here I interrupted him and asked surprisingly, was your journey so smooth?

No, definitely not, he smiled.

He then shared what kind of problems he faced in his practice and how he came out of it. He, like most of us had health concerns, family issues, and also faced some legal problem once, but those were tough times, which he faced strongly and came out of. He shared what decisions went wrong and what went well. All in all, it was not an easy journey for him and he worked hard to reach a position where people saw him as a wealthy, rich and renowned doctor. After telling his story, he specifically said, that now that I knew how hard he worked to reach this stage in life, he expected me to manage his money properly so that it could be safe with no compromise on growth.

He asked me advice on multibagger stocks to multiply his wealth fast. After listening to his story, it was my turn to take him on the real investment ride. I explained that if the wealth generation exercise were so easy, then why would anyone have a need to work hard? Why not just figure out few "multibagger stocks" and just watch your wealth grow? Moreover, multibaggers are called multibaggers only after they have already delivered supernatural returns. It's incredibly difficult to find one in the first place, but you will always find them in hindsight.

No one can ever predict in advance which is going to be the next one, and even if someone zeros down on something, sometimes it takes decades for that stock to actually show a multibagger potential. Moreover, due to market movements, many times investors do not enjoy its potential to the fullest and come out of it at a very early stage.

I told him quite seriously, "Saurabh, you are no less than a multibagger to me, and after looking at your bank balances, I feel that if I had opted for medical science and not commerce, I would have such a fat bank balance too! But now since I have heard your story, I can understand how hard you worked in your past years to reach this level. For those who are just looking at your wealth and roaring practice, to them, you are just another rich doctor and they may strive to become like you, without knowing that it took 20 years for you to reach this stage or be called as 'multibagger'.

Making money from investments is no different from setting up a business or practice. But when you look at the investments from the past returns perspective only, you tend to ignore the process of investing. You need to have discipline, the same kind of patience and perseverance, that you displayed in your profession. Just like your profession or your employment, you could also experience some bad phases in your investment journey. But when your goals are clear and you are in the right direction, then you face such phases with confidence. You know that you are investing for a bigger objective and these hiccups are part of the journey. And after some years, you can call those phases as learning and experiences."

I continued, "Saurabh, you started off with a government job, just because you felt you had to gain experience and more practical knowledge on your subject. Those 6 years also helped you in building a strong client base, which helped you in setting up your practice. You could have made more money in your initial work life too if you were into your own practice but the objective was to be a good doctor, so you delayed the gratification and invested your 6 years in developing your professional self. You took the time to learn, and made the foundation strong before taking the plunge."

As the saying goes – good things come to those who wait.

Saurabh listened to me intently. I explained, "In investments too, you should strive to be a good investor, rather than searching for good investments.

You are already making money, but the purpose of investments should be to convert your money to your wealth, which helps you achieve your life goals comfortably and live peacefully.

Learning never stops in any profession. You also attend many conferences, read books to stay updated with recent changes in medical science, which means that you have to keep investing in yourself to keep your worth intact. By continuously investing in yourself, you have reached that stage where regular income is not an issue, in financial terms we call it a present value (As I explained in The Formula of Success). You have made yourself so worthy that come what may, no economic slowdown, no recession can impact your income, unlike other professions. It's now that you just need to put your income in the right direction, by giving it the adequate time to get the future value that you want.

You have been investing in your life for the past so many years, now you can ask for the withdrawal and do good for yourself and others in your life. You have been running for the past 20 years. Now is the time to pause and reflect, to make wise decisions, decisions to make money work for you. Your investment success is a reflection of how you lead your personal and professional life. If you are calm, patient and disciplined, then you can turn any investment into a multibagger.

Look deeper into yourself to get all the answers. No

one has ever achieved success in short time, and as they say that it's not timing the market but time in the market that leads you to desired results."

Beware of Social Proof

What did you think of Saurabh's story? Exciting? Inspiring? Boring? Or is there nothing new about it? Whichever way you have found it, it was his story, Saurabh's story and he is not YOU.

You are different from him, you are different from your friends, your siblings, your neighbours; your needs, desires, income, expenses, aspirations, liabilities, responsibilities are all different. So, what you have to do is bring your focus back to your own story. However, it is important to remember the advice I gave Saurabh, as that is the mantra to turn your life into a multibagger. It's all about investing the time, health and money in the right manner. Generally, people are worried about the third factor and ignore the first two.

Do you remember the last time you checked out traveller/buyers' reviews before booking any hotel or doing online shopping? You do it most of the time if not always, right? After all, if there are many reviews, it shows that the product has been bought by many others, and when those reviews are positive with an above average rating, this gives you the confidence that those using it are happy with it.

You tend to download the mobile app having more

comparable number of downloads with other similar apps, or at least those apps which your friend circle is using (recommendations). If most of your friends have an iPhone, how you can settle for a Micromax? You feel safe when your kids get into some engineering or medical college, even if they want to study social sciences, after all this is what most kids do. When most of your colleagues drive an SUV, you feel down owning a sedan. When they go to Europe for holidays and you to Himachal, you feel that you may not have grown that much in life. In the same way how many times have you invested in or shown interest in a mutual fund or any other security, just because that investment has generated good returns for your friend, colleague or family member? THINK!

This particular behavioural phenomenon is known as "Social proof" or "Herd behaviour", which dictates that individuals feel they are behaving correctly when they act the same like other people. In other words, if they are doing something opposite to what others are doing, they feel uncomfortable and unsafe or left out. We feel safe with the group and often ignore our feelings and likings in the process.

Social influence is a powerful force in nature and society. In many cases it's not bad at all. It may ensure that you watch a good movie, visit a great restaurant, travel to a brand-new place or save you from dangerous situations. However, the challenge is in evaluating personal beliefs when they contradict what others are doing. The result is that groups evolve to be unresponsive to changes in their environment and spend too much time copying one another, and not making their own decisions.

Marketers know how to play with this mindset. So, when some sales person tells you that "next door Sharma Ji" has also bought this or invested in this, then to avoid the feeling of being left behind, you also buy the same. Amazon tells you that "those who've bought "this" also have bought "that". You were shown some ladies saying why they prefer a specific toothpaste over others, to give you a feeling that your choice is among the popular products and you are not alone. They bring someone with a white coat to make you believe that you are getting a recommendation from a doctor/expert. Celebrities/public figures endorsing brands give you a recall factor. All these are examples of promoting something with a "Social Proof".

Why Do You Need Social Proof?

In the ancient times, following others or moving in herds was a good survival strategy. It provided a kind of sense of security from predators. To save one self from animal attacks or to plan to attack on animals for food, tribes needed to move in groups. Those who acted differently from the group, exited the gene pool. We are the direct descendants of those who copied others' behaviour. This pattern is so deeply rooted in us that we still use it today, even when it offers no survival advantage.

Social Proof and your Investments

Now think about your investments. You have a good allocation in equity, and suddenly you get a WhatsApp message with bad news which says that markets are expecting a big fall tomorrow; you call your friend who had suggested some of your investment choices and he says that he has already withdrawn his investments. Moreover, all his other friends whom he advised on these investments have also exited. What would you do? How would you react to this? Would you panic? Would you also like to withdraw your savings the first thing the next morning, because everyone else around you has done it or has plans to do it? Even if you know that your goals are 10 years away from today?

You want to buy residential property not because you need a house to live in, but because all your friends have already bought their houses. In fact, they have two more which they have put on rent. Everyone around you is buying gold as they feel that this will never come down or is an ever-growing investment, so you also get tempted to buy some.

I keep getting queries for suggestions on "best Systematic Investment Plan (SIP)" with a long-term time horizon. And long term for them is 3 years. On asking why they want SIP, they reply that SIP is a better tool than a recurring deposit and these days' people prefer SIPs more than any other investment, and this is what they've been reading everywhere.

Without understanding that SIP is just a mode of investment and it doesn't nullify the risks prevalent in the market, even risk-averse investors want to have exposure to equity SIPs, even with a short (long) term horizon.

If you look at the past data of investor's exposure in the stock markets in 2007-08, you will find that the highest equity allocation by retail investors was in end 2007 i.e. when they saw everyone making money around them and wanted to take advantage of "India's growth story". Rather than following the principle of "buy low and sell high", you have a tendency of "buy high and sell low", as that is the time when you find other people are doing the same thing. As I said many times earlier, you are victim of your own behaviour and looking for Social proof is one of the cognitive biases, which does not let you focus on YOU. Sellers and even the media play around with this behaviour by creating excitement or a sense of fear and greed through different articles and selling techniques.

How to Avoid the Trap of Social Proof

In childhood your teachers and parents must have sometimes asked you, "Woh agar chhat se chalaang lagayega to tum bhi lagaoge kya?" (if someone jumps from a roof would you follow him?) That was the perfect question to ask why do you want to follow the other person blindly? When many people do the same thing that may not mean that is the wise thing to do. If a survey says most of the readers like to read a particular magazine then that does not mean it carries the articles which you may also like, if one mutual fund has highest AUM then that may not suit your goal.

These are my few cents which may help you avoid falling in the social proof trap, with reference to investment management.

1. Know "WHY"

Before falling for any sales pitch or reacting to market news (good/bad) you need to understand the WHY behind it. WHY have you invested or WHY should you invest/withdraw, in/from this product? Do you already have some goals where this product is fitting in or has this product made you realize that you need to have some goals? If the latter is true then this is the time to work on your goals rather than making investments. For example, understand what is more important for a comfortable retirement. Buying a pension plan or doing proper retirement planning to then see if a pension plan fits into it?

Answer this simple question: Are you investing or withdrawing from a particular investment after a well thought of strategy and the decision is part of your long-term plan, or you are just reacting to market noise? Pause and reflect.

2. Ask "WHY"

When you are sure on your "WHY", then now is the

time to understand other people's "WHY". This is where you need to understand that it is none of your business to know what is happening in other people's lives. Their reaction may be due to a lot many reasons better known to them. You can only control your behaviour and not theirs.

But yes, if you are being pitched to by some sales person then you should know WHY he is advising what he is advising. And also, WHY he is advising to YOU? WHY does he feel that what he's advising is good advice for YOU? Here you will find out that you will not get sound advice from someone who is not aware about your financials, your goals, your requirements, and these are some things which cannot be discussed with every Tom, Dick and Harry.

3. Put yourself in a process through Financial Planning

A financial plan is person specific. It does not take into consideration what others are doing, but what is best for you. It will put you in a process and if followed well, eliminate most of the biases; It makes you invest in suitable products too considering your risk profile and aspirations. Even a SIP puts you into a process, but with the wrong understanding, having no hold on cash flows and also with no plan in place, most SIPs die young. So, a comprehensive financial plan is very important, which not only takes care of your investments and asset allocation, but also has a well-defined strategy towards your long- and short-term goals and answers all possible "What if" scenarios.

4. Take help of financial planners

You have to have a professional financial planner by your side. A human who understands human emotions, not a machine which does what you want it to do; a human who counters your thoughts, understands or questions the WHY behind your action and guides you on necessary steps. I've observed in many situations, the best thing that one should do is to relax, sit quietly and wait for the mayhem or excitement to get over. Here investors get overpowered by their emotions and feel like they should do something like invest more or withdraw immediately. But a professional by your side can help you sail through these mood swings.

Conclusion

> "While we are free to choose our actions, we are not free to choose the consequences of our actions" – **Stephen R. Covey**

Before saying, I'll have what he's having, ask yourself a few questions. Decisions which others are taking for their investment may not be good for your financial health. Understand that you are a different person with different requirements. Don't let sellers take advantage of your weakness for social proof. Be sceptical, whenever a company claims its product is better because it is the "most popular".

You may buy a specific product based on another

buyer's review, but your purchasing decisions should not depend on what others are buying. Same goes with investments. For spending be aware of your budget and for investment be aware of your financial plan. All these multibaggers, best investments, star rankings etc. all are in the past; you have to be prepared and take good care of your future.

It's easy to stand with the crowd, it takes courage to stand alone. Do what you think is right for you and not what others are doing.

CHALLENGE YOUR BELIEFS

Challenge Your Beliefs

In a TED talk, psychologist Jennice Vilhauer asked the audience to raise their hands if they wanted to win a lottery ticket. Almost everyone raised their hands. She later said to keep their hands raised if they bought a lottery ticket in the last month. All hands went down. She later concluded that this is because they did not "expect" to win the lottery, which is why they did not buy the tickets, yet everyone "wants" to win the lottery. She explained that people act based on what they expect, not what they want. And they do not act if they do not expect.

Expectation is a belief of whether or not you are going to get what you want.

Losing weight is something that you may want, but when you do not expect that you could lose weight then you would not, as that belief would not let you to act. Your thoughts would not allow you to hit the gym, go on a jog or control your diet. Time and again your mind will give you some excuses to avoid action. Like my job does not allow me to, I do not get time, there is too much pollution out there, I have read that dieting does not help much in losing weight, it's a hereditary problem etc. You will give full justification and strong reasons, due to a belief that it will not work in your case.

You want your child to be a good human being, but

you do not act on it, because you expect others to work on it as you think this is not your job. You may say that this is the school's Job and you can only put him into a good school. Or you may say your child spends most of the time with his/her mother/father so s/he should take care of his behaviour.

You want to have financial freedom, you want to be successful in life, you want to live in peace, you want to have a perfect investment portfolio, you want to have a work life balance, you want to have a healthy lifestyle...but if you do not expect to get it, you will not get it.

Expectation + Actions = creation of life experiences

You do not act on what you want, but on what you expect; like on what you believe can happen. If you don't believe or don't keep faith in your better future, you will always keep struggling in life. But if you believe or expect that your future is going to be better than today then you will definitely act on it and make it a reality. Many times, you just want and put your expectation on outer things which are not in your control, so it does not call for any action on your side. And now the outcome would depend on how better the other person does that work and with what belief and attitude.

I remember when I was about to start my financial planning practice and actually struggling to find ways to work, at that time I got in touch with some senior planners of the industry through LinkedIn (a professional networking site) and formed an association. We planned to have monthly calls, webinars and many other activities so the members of the group could learn and gain from each other. Suresh, the mentor of the group, once called for a meeting in Mumbai and specifically told all those who were coming, to read the book Secret and watch the movie Karate Kid, before coming over.

The book is about law of attraction, which says that when you think of the things you want in life and you focus on them with all your intention, then the universe will give you exactly what you want. It also says that when you think of something that you don't want to happen, and thus move your focus to those things, then those will also happen. It says that the universe doesn't understand the word "Don't", "Not", or "No".

We used to think that once we become a CFP, then life will be set and we will keep getting clients on a regular basis without doing much effort. After all financial planning is the need of the hour and there's so much mis-selling happening around and people are frustrated with sellers and looking for trustworthy planners.

Suresh clarified, referring to the book Secret, that it's good to have a strong belief about the future as that is the only thing that keeps us positive and gets us going, but until you act on the same you will not be able to see it. You have to be sure of your efforts and do it in the best possible manner, you will get the results. But there is no time line to the results. You just have to keep working.

Don't expect that people will not deal with product sellers, they will not buy wrong investment products as this is all out of your control; instead work on your domain and make yourself strong in what you do. As by not expecting them to do what they're currently doing, you are diverting your attention from the important thing, which is your goal.

And it's not about the certification, its more about character, honesty and integrity as people will be trusting us for their financial future. So, do what you should to remain relevant to them.

"First learn stand, then learn fly. Nature rule, Daniel-san, not mine" – Mr. Miyagi (Karate Kid)

Result-oriented actions require commitment, perseverance, patience and process, which we learnt from the Karate Kid movie. That session was kind of a belief calibrator for us. It's not about having knowledge or a certification, but what you do with your knowledge is what that matters. Having a belief about a good future is great, as it guides your action, but you should always remain open minded and keep updating your beliefs and knowledge, to remain relevant in an ever-changing economy and industry.

Buying a lottery ticket does not guarantee winning, but not buying it guarantees losing.

Beliefs shape our lives. Beliefs make or break our future. Beliefs guide us how to live. It defines our personality, our character. It impacts our thoughts and influences our decision making.

Everything that you do or not do is because of your beliefs. Whatever qualification you have or profession you are in today, is because of your belief. Either you had a belief or were made to believe by your parents, teachers or friends that this is the best education for you. You always invest in real estate as you have a belief that the stock market is a gamble and since you have never made money whenever you invested in shares, so you formed one more belief that it is not meant for you. Or you never preferred a specific investment asset due to your inexperience or bad experience or the stories that you have heard.

Beliefs are formed with experiences, inferences and deductions or what others have told us. Though it is an age old saying that seeing is believing, but in this information age no one has time to experience or see things in real, but they hear or read to believe it to be true. Since ancient times we have been forming beliefs by seeing and hearing. It is reasonable to presume that our senses are not lying. In fact, questioning what you see or hear in those times could have got you eaten. In other words, better to be safe than sorry, especially when considering whether to believe that the rustling in the grass is a lion or not!

Most of the beliefs we form has its root in childhood, by seeing, hearing and believing our parents, school teachers and friends. When we were born, our mind was a clean slate and whatever impression and understanding of the world we got at that time had a long-lasting impact on us and played a big role in forming our beliefs. Sometimes you were told to believe or many times you inferred the same by yourself. If you have seen your parents struggling to make ends meet, then you may have a belief that money is important and hard to earn or you may infer that money is bad, since it keeps you away from your loved ones as they spent most of their time in earning money. If you were told that it is love that is more important and money is always secondary, then you may have a different impression of the situation.

One of my doctor friend's son who was studying in Class 9th, said to me that its ok not to pay income taxes. And when I asked him what does he know about income taxes so he very vaguely answered that it's the portion of your hard-earned income you have to pay to the government. It's a kind of "hafta" that the government asks for. Now you may guess who formed such an impression and belief in his mind. Those were definitely not of his own.

As we grow old, go to school, meet new people, we get influenced by a new environment and set of places. Many times, we had an impression and belief of what our teachers had taught us in school. Regular preaching, scolding, bullying by other kids, high grade, low grade, everything leaves an impression in kids mind and impacts their self-confidence and forms their beliefs. If kids are regularly scolded by teachers for not doing well in studies and they hear the same kind of words from their parents, then they may form a belief that they can never do well in life. With this low self-esteem when they go into a job and don't perform well, they will hear such words again from the boss too, which puts them in a vicious circle of low confidence and low performance.

In the current age of mobile apps and fast news flow, we believe everything and anything that we hear and consider it to be true. This is not all, we also share the same with others, without even vetting the correctness of the same. I am sure you must be receiving many such stupid messages on your WhatsApp and other social media accounts, shared by someone whom you were expecting to be a wise person. And even sometimes you too, without vetting the information, just forward it to other friends. Sharing is considered as endorsing. And you endorse something only when you believe it to be true.

It happens, as this is one of the oldest ways you have been forming your beliefs. You hear something and believe it to be true. It is only sometimes later or when asked about the source or correctness of the info, then you spend time and search for the same to find out if it is true or false.

This is the default setting since the age of evolution. But still many do not agree with this and say they don't believe what they hear or read, and that they first vet that and then accept the info. It is hard to accept what you are doing currently is wrong as this in turn is kind of challenging your belief about what you do.

- The more you hear of stories of people making or losing money in stock markets, the more your belief about stock markets (on positives or negatives) strengthens.
- The more you read stories on how insurance companies have not paid out claims to the insured, the more you believe that insurance companies are not trustworthy. If you hear a story of a friend who experienced such a situation, your belief gets stronger.
- The more you hear stories on SIPs as a wonderful product for long term investing, the stronger you believe that this is the right way of investment.
- The more you hear bad news about someone getting cheated by some financial advisor, insurance agents, the stronger your belief gets that it's better to do it yourself.
- The more you hear benefits of financial planning, the stronger your belief grow about this structured process.

The more you think good, the more you believe good and get good.

Challenge Your Beliefs and Manage Your Expectations

We don't see things as they are...we see things as we are. You must be thinking that it's not only what we hear or read, but what we experience also leads to belief formation and thus forms expectations about the future. This is true but as Aldous Huxley said, "Experience is not what happens to a man, it is what a man does with what happens to him." The brain works on the principle of anticipation. We try to project the results much before it occurs.

In anticipation we mostly think of the rewards. Rewards means all the things that will make your life worth living. When you anticipate to get rewards you get happiness, excitement, but when you do not anticipate any rewards you feel sadness, disappointment. Anticipation sounds similar to expectation but actually is the initial stage of expectation. I read somewhere the difference between anticipation and expectation is that anticipation is what you hope for, and expectation is what you think you are entitled to. Your initial experience with something may be the result of your anticipation, but with the results that you got out of that is what you have started believing as you are entitled to.

That's where in many cases we cling to our past. We use the past to project the future. If you have failed once you might think you will fail again. Or you may take it to heart and want to achieve it at all costs even if that results in failing to achieve other goals.

Let me explain. You have started with a new job and are earning well. You have no experience of making investments. You hear from your colleagues around that mutual funds are the best way to invest for future and some said that it is direct stocks that make money fast. You were not having a clear idea, so you decided not to invest anywhere but observe first and then decide. Also, you tried to learn both by googling and read many articles on these subjects. Some say SIPs are better, some say stocks are better.

After a few months, you decided to go with SIPs, by anticipating good returns. You keep saving for 1 year and see that SIPs have not generated good returns whereas stock investors are minting money. You stop your SIPs and start investing in stocks. You have no finance background, neither do you know how to do stock analysis, but you invest in some stocks with whatever readings you can do and make money.

Now you start reading more and also start believing that your reading of the newspaper and articles, is the research that you're supposed to do before investing in stocks. And also, you are a great stock investor. After all you are making money and thus all the credit should go to you. Now you feel returns are something you are entitled to earn with this kind of research and form a belief around your expertise. After some years, you experience a big fall in the stock market and find most of your shares bleeding. The economy slowed down and you lost your job too.

Since most of your investments were in direct stocks which have reduced to more than half, and you have no other savings, so you booked the losses and redeemed all your money. The SIPs were also in equity funds, so they also were down. There could be some stocks which were well researched and was also a good investment to keep, but sometimes markets do not differentiate good and bad business in the fall, so they fell In line with the overall downtrend. You still had confidence in your stock picking ability and took the risk of further investing by taking some soft loans from family. But since the slowdown extended to a few years and you had no patience (as you had never experienced such a slow growth earlier), you once again booked losses.

This disappointing experience has such a big impact on your mind that you form a new belief that the stock market is a gamble and only big players make money here. Everything is manipulated. This is a true story of many investors, written in a few short lines, but extending across many years. This belief you have formed was about your investments only, but not about your research, not about the way of investing and the process you follow. You had no emergency fund in place, no back up of insurance, no asset allocation approach, no diversification. You went with your belief and ignored the basic fundamentals of the investment process. This self-serving bias of calling your work as skill and results as luck is natural. Whatever good has happened is because of your efforts, but all that was bad was due to luck or other people's misdoings. In 'others' you have government, employer, spouse, kids, neighbours, colleagues and what not.

But the problem could be in the process too. Bad research, wrong belief on investment returns to start with, lack of understanding of the asset class. The pattern of blaming others for bad outcomes and failing to give credit for good ones is all over the place. When someone else at work gets a promotion instead of us, we never admit that the person has really worked hard or deserved the job, more than we did. We say it was because the boss was partial.

If someone does better in school, it was because the teacher likes them more. If our car meets with an accident it was always because of another person's fault. When you are making money in the markets it was your skill, and when it went into losses it was because of the advisor, markets, governments.

Dan Ariely, a psychologist and behavioural economist in his book Predictably Irrational says that the way we file the outcomes is predictably patterned. We take credit for the good stuff and blame the bad stuff on luck so it won't be our fault. The result is that we don't learn from experience well. Beliefs are formed from outcomes which could be the result of luck or skill or both. Every outcome has some learning in it and we need to accept it. There is a big difference in getting the experience and becoming an expert. Expertise lies in the ability to identify the teachings hidden in every outcome, and learn the lessons out of it. Every experience can be different, and happiness lies in expecting the unexpected out of every experience. Experience can be an effective teacher. But, clearly only some students listen to their teachers.

If your experience has been as expected, then try to learn how it could have been better, and what factors worked in it well: was it luck or skill? And if the experience was not good, then it has given you an opportunity to find out the mistakes and learn more. For example, in investments, mistakes could be in the form of mis-buying not mis-selling, not asking correct questions in the first place, not reviewing at regular intervals, becoming over-enthusiastic in the stock markets and so on. Every outcome is a feedback.

Experiencing the same results every time may make your beliefs stubborn and you stop noticing the evidence confirming the opposite. But there is always the other side of the coin too and you should be open minded. Smartness is not always in being right, but in accepting that something is there which is missing or may need some improvement. If we can find ways to become more comfortable with uncertainty, we can see the world more accurately and be better with it.

You have to keep challenging your beliefs. Rather than finding and reading something which confirms your belief, sometimes you should also try to find the opposite side of it.

Ask Google, it will tell you everything you want to read. Ask your experiences, what has gone well and what went wrong. Take professional help. Sometimes you need some other person to tell you where you are going wrong. The other person could be a financial planner, spouse, a friend.

A good life is one with few anxieties. Most of your life's stress comes from the gap between expectation and reality. Larger the gap between what you expect and what you want, the more distress you feel. You want a healthy and happy life, but you expect you will get it only by having more money, a bigger house, luxury car and what not. You act on what you expect, but do not get what you want, as in the process of accumulating things you forget about life.

What you expect is a dream, what you want is reality. But that should not stop you from dreaming or expecting.

See there are two ways to understand this. To keep yourself away from distress you have two options. Either forget what you expect, ignore it and give up or you can change your expectations to match with you want and take consistent actions to achieve it. Goals should come from your life i.e. what you want and then you should start building expectations around it as to how you would like to see yourself in it.

If every actor expects to become Shahrukh Khan, then that may lead to disappointment for many. But if one understands what he truly wants and understands the meaning of becoming a good actor then one may strive to become likes of Rajkumar Rao, Nawazuddin Siddique, Richa Chaddha, Divya Dutta etc.

In the same way every investor cannot become Warren Buffet. But if you want to become a good investor then you may strive to learn his investment strategies, patience and discipline. Look at your life holistically. When you lay down a plan in front of you, you begin to see the possibilities. Wants are looking inside and expectations are always looking outside.

Sometimes your expectations are because of your stature, reputation, job profile, your income, your family background...as in you may say a person of your cadre doesn't drive small cars or that you are a family of doctors and your children should also be doctors only. Your past may be the reason of where you are, but your future is something you can design on your own, it's just that you have to look into the eyes of your beliefs and challenge it wherever required. Do not let wrong expectations and beliefs put limits on your future.

In fact, expectations are not bad but getting attached to them is definitely not good. When you are too tied to the specific results you can't be in the present moment. According to Robert Kegan, a Harvard psychologist, the only way to truly experience the highest levels of transformation and "conscious evolution" is to detach from the need for specific outcomes. Although outcomes are important, they are something which you cannot control. What you can do is set realistic goals which comes from what you think you should achieve, not what you think others want you to achieve, commit to it with a set process, plan for it, review the plan time and again and tweak it wherever necessary.

> Learn and unlearn in the process. Challenge your beliefs more often to make your life and money journey smooth and enjoyable.

OVERCOMING THE DIFFICULTY IN BEING GOOD

Overcoming the Difficulty in Being Good

Ok, so we are at the last chapter of this book.

If you have gone through all the chapters carefully and if I was able to explain clearly, you must have got the gist of the book, which is all about being good. Be it your relationships, your friends, your employer, government and even your money, all want you to be good.

Actually, good is your first nature but due to past bad experiences, behaviour biases, the beliefs that you have formed, the confusion between needs and desires, not focusing on what you really want, you have just been compromising with your goodness. You just forgot the way to happiness and ignored the freedom you truly enjoy, and also have stopped appreciating the success you have got in life.

Being good is appreciating and enjoying what you have and also about sincerely working towards what you really want and expect from your work and life, by following a system and taking all the stakeholders along. Money plays a very important role in your life; in fact, it is one of your most important relationships. Like every good relationship, it also demands respect and attention from your side, to reciprocate in the same way. Just as you expect someone to be happy in your success and also stand by you in the times of distress, similarly your money will always be there for your help, provided you have treated it in the same way in the past.

To help money help you, you have to have deposits in your accounts. The deposits which you have accumulated by showing respect to your money, nurturing it, protecting it, saving it and showing it the way to grow. Every relationship expects this from you. You have to have good deposits with them lying in an emotional bank account so as to withdraw it at a later stage with comfort, ease and no distress. Your personal relationships demand deposits of love, affection, attention and care. You will always get love from your loved ones if you give them love. You will get attention and time from your friends and family members if you stood by them in their time of need. You will keep getting the respect from your employer, colleagues if you have never treated them badly. This is the way money wants you to treat it, if you really want to achieve your goals and be prepared for emergencies and live RICH.

In Section 2: Knowing of this book, I have explained the way to be responsible towards your money and how to build that into your habit, so as to keep track of it and also to understand what could be the important areas you may require money's help in, by deciding on the important goals. I have also discussed the different kind of risks you need to cope with, out of which some are manageable and some are not. And since you yourself can be a risk to your money and investment portfolio, it is better to take a professional's help here. Yes, it is important because I know and you also agree with me, that even after reading this book, you cannot immediately stop doing comparisons and challenge your beliefs. You may need hand holding, you may need someone to tell you what you are doing wrong and what can be done in a different way.

This is the main reason that even I have a financial planner who keeps guiding me on my way so I do not derail from the path to wellbeing. But it does not mean that you cannot do it yourself. I am a professional in this field, but after spending many years with my money and also handling many client accounts, I have always felt that it is better to keep your own money management in the hands of someone else as it is quite natural to get emotional towards your investment decisions. Also, there are many other areas in life which demand more attention, which I may ignore if I give my spare time to things that can be outsourced.

You tend to spend on unwanted things; it is human to be greedy sometimes especially when the question is about making money, social media does not let you stay in peace and is the major source that makes you compare yourself with the world, the news around does not let you enjoy and stick to the process, and many other things where you end up compromising your goodness. You need a guide and mentor to help you keep away from all this clutter.

Staying ahead, not staying together, has slowly become the mantra of a so-called successful life, and this uncalled-for pressure lets you compromise with your integrity and basic good character.

So, is there any solution? Can you still be good in this complicated and demanding world?

Yes, there are a few solutions, which if practiced well can get you the answer to lots of your problems, and get you a good, productive and wealthy life. Let's start with NO.

Goodness is in Saying NO

Are you a YES person? Do you like to please everyone around you by accepting all their offers and even buy the products they sell? Do you say YES to every samosa party happening in your office? Do you say YES to every online sale and then the EMI offers by credit cards? Do you say YES to all the new iPhone launches? And do you say YES to all these, even after knowing their ill effects on your life and money?

When you know what is distracting you from your path, then why is it so difficult to say NO to them?

Yes, there are some instances where it becomes tough, especially when you are dealing with known people. But you can make it easy when you know your priorities well and understand that you cannot do it all. And if the other people are your true well-wishers, then they would not feel bad at your NO and will understand that you are on another important mission which when completed will ultimately benefit all, as they are also part of your life. It is imperative for you to know that when you are saying YES to one thing you are saying NO to the other. You may have your justification for this but if that "Other" is more important to your life goals then you are doing great injustice to yourself.

It's up to you to decide what's more important to you.

- When you say yes to spending, you say no to saving
- When you say yes to endowment insurance plans, you say no to other flexible products like mutual funds
- When you say yes to insurance expenses, you say no to a financial planner fee
- When you say yes to a samosa, you say no to salads
- When you say yes to your friends' party, you say no to a cricket match with your kid
- When you say yes to TV you say no to reading

However, when you think of the things you could do by saying NO to the one in front of you, you may feel less guilty and more productive.

Your work life is important, but this does not mean that you keep saying NO to all the things in your personal life to please your bosses or colleagues in order to build a fake rapport with the aim of getting a promotion and earn more. Also, you just can't say NO to your work every time when you have guests at home. You need to balance between your personal and professional life, which requires the need to be clear on your priorities first.

The whole idea of saying NO to something is to gain complete focus on important things.

Focusing requires fewer distractions and less on your plate. Be it any area of your life – work, personal, financial, family and spiritual – to get extraordinary results you have to work with focus. And your focus should be on important things which are aligned with your purpose in life. You need to prioritize as then only you can generate productivity and profit from your work. Focusing is a habit which needs to be developed. Research has proved that multitasking is a myth and leads to compromising with efficiency. Focusing is less about saying YES, but more about saying NO, as without NO, YES cannot exist. The real question here though is, how do you say NO without offending the other party or in the worst case, losing your job?

In the book *The One Thing*, the authors Gary Keller and Jay Papasan have very beautifully explained the importance of doing one thing at a time, as this only will give that thing enough focus and importance that it deserves. They say messes are inevitable when you focus on just one thing. If you want to get your most important thing done, then it is guaranteed that other things may get compromised.

For example, when you are really serious about buying a new house and it is very important to your and your family's happiness, then you focus purely on saving towards that goal. And in this you may have to compromise on your vacations which may irk your kids, you may not buy your wife her birthday gift, you won't be able to attend some family get togethers, or you may not be able to replace your old furniture.

What is important is important. **This is why it is essential that you do the exercises that I set in Section 2.** The exercises give you a holistic view of what is important and needs attention in your lives. You can very easily set your goals and priorities after that, which will need your complete focus to achieve them. Chaos is normal when you give your attention to only one thing and ignore the other. And it is imperative to accept it and manage it well. You need to be creative and open to deal with it. While it is important to learn to manage the probable chaos around you, there are some things which you can't ignore.

No one succeeds alone and no one fails alone. Remember – ***"Hum hi hum hai to kya hum hai, tum hi tum ho to kya tum ho."***

Pay attention to people around you. Your environment, which includes the people surrounding you and also your physical surroundings, must support your goal. This could be the time you need to withdraw some of your love and care deposits which you have accumulated in your relationships. You have to make your immediate family understand the importance of the one thing for you and how this will impact everyone's life. If you have true friends then they will definitely understand your "No". Goodness lies in great and effective communication. You have to make your employer understand why you need flexible working hours, what you are trying to achieve and how that thing will help you and your company's growth.

There has to be a win/win for every stakeholder. And if you are true and sincere to this then you don't need a technique to communicate effectively to the other person. It would reflect in your character. The truth in your words, the passion in your action, the honesty in your eyes. Stephen Covey in his book *7 Habits of Highly Effective People*, says win/win sees life as cooperative and not competitive, and is based on a paradigm that there's plenty for everybody. Win/Win is a belief in the third alternative. It's not your way or my way; it's a better way, a higher way. Being with like-minded people will bring a positive change in your life and increase your focus on important things.

Chaos can be managed until a certain level, but if it goes beyond your head then it can have serious implications. So, make people around you understand the sensitivity and importance of your actions, but don't let yourself surrender to your environment. The right people in your life and right surroundings will support your efforts to get the One Thing.

Switch Off the Loudspeakers Around You

Besides the goodness of saying No to many trivial things and to focus on the important ones, you should also have to learn to filter the voices from the noise around. In the book The Art of the Good Life, Rolf Dobelli has referenced an experiment once conducted by Canadian researchers on sparrows.

To give the sparrows a safer environment from the variety of natural predators – racoons, owls, falcons etc, researchers decided to block off a whole area of the forest with nets, shutting out the sparrows' natural enemies. Then the researchers dotted the forest with hidden loudspeakers. In one area of the woods, they played the noise of predators and in the other, non-threatening natural sounds. The results showed that sparrows which were exposed to the "bad" noises, laid 40% fewer eggs with smaller than average sizes, and fewer of them hatched. Many of the chicks starved to death because their parents were too afraid to forage for food, and the surviving chicks were weaker. The experiment clearly showed that it doesn't even take a real threat to influence a whole ecosystem - fear is enough.

What goes for sparrows also goes for human beings. Worse still, we are not just afraid of predators but a lot many other things. In fact, the majority of our worries are superfluous as the problem that is turning in your mind is not that dangerous or it is something you cannot do anything about.

- Will I get a promotion this year?
- Will my child score well in her exams?
- Parents are not keeping well
- My cholesterol levels are going high
- Can I save enough for my retirement?
- Stock market fluctuations
- Interest rates movements

...are some of the areas which worry you in your personal life. This is not all, some people's worries are related to the outside world, like politics, global warming, geopolitical tensions, sports, neighbours or relatives. Some of the worry is real, which may have come from your past experiences, observation, but many times it's just imaginary. For example, a stock market fall is real but that it will start falling only when you start investing in is imaginary. Death is real, but you will die after writing a will or buying life insurance is imaginary. Some say financial planning always fails in my case, I am not that structured person.

The major causes of worry are fear of the unknown, trying to control the uncontrollable, wrong expectations and comparisons. We all have many loudspeakers around us in the form of relatives, colleagues, neighbours who keep on edging in with their experiences, stories and suggestions to confuse us.

You may have decided to say NO to many but there are still some loudspeakers that you turn on yourself, and the major one is Google. You treat Google as your best advisor and seek out every answer from it. Without appreciating the fact that Google is only a search engine, which may take you to the content and information you are seeking, but using that information wisely requires knowledge and experience.

In your financial life, there are many different loudspeakers, which rather than easing your worry increase it, which further results in indecisiveness and stress, making you lose focus on what is important for you. Some of them are business newspapers, business news channels, Google, Facebook, Twitter, WhatsApp groups, blogs etc. When you do not have any structure in place, you easily lose your focus on the stories being shared in these newspapers, news channels and other social media. You start believing that these are your stories and if you do the same thing as advised in it, you may achieve your goals too.

This is not the right approach to money management. You should treat them as a place of information, not as advice. And keep in mind that 80% of the information you read is useless to you. The remaining 20% can be used to improve 80% of your life. The remaining 20% of life is about accepting and letting go.

Try to understand that most of the voices around you are only noise and you should not confuse what's new with what's relevant. Distraction is in the air, and it is up to you how you keep yourself away from all of them. The time you spend on your social media posts is part of your limited time which you would have better invested on resolving your concerns and worries to make your future better. The attention you are giving to your WhatsApp messages or TV shows is the attention you are taking away from the person sitting in front of you. Every new product, breaking news, multibagger suggestion, opinion, Facebook and Instagram post wants an audience and the moment we read it we pay – in focus and time. Clear away these distractions. Watch less TV, avoid technology that is FREE, read more (information is best absorbed in written form) and avoid websites that are full of third-party ads.

Know what matters and what you can control. Many times, we keep on worrying about those things which may matter to us but are not in our control, and this creates unnecessary stress in our minds which in turn affect our efficiency and also health.

Referring to the worries I mentioned earlier, although promotion is important it is not in your control; what you can only do is work efficiently and honestly. How your child would score in her exams is not in your control; what you can only do is get her quality education, help her clear the doubts she has and support and encourage her efforts. Your parents' health is important, but you cannot control it. You can support them, give them a healthier and happier environment, help and support them in taking regular medicines, get regular health check-ups done and take care of them. It happens in your financial life too.

Although a financial plan is important and it definitely matters a lot, you have to understand that it is based on a few assumptions like inflation, rate of return etc. which are not in anyone's control. Not even stock market fluctuations or interest rate movements can be controlled.

What you can control is the process aspect of it. You can create a well-defined process, by understanding all the what-ifs and the best- and worst-case scenarios. You may keep it flexible enough to manage any kind of emergency, you may do all the analysis to find out what products may suit you best. But after that you just keep following the process, be disciplined in your savings and keep on monitoring and reviewing; the rest will be automatically taken care of.

Review the plan and process time and again. Spending time on searching for best investments that can make you wealthy is just a waste. I keep receiving many queries on good health insurance, life insurance policies, or which company has a good claim ratio, low premium, good customer service and what not. And I make it clear that though knowing all these things are important and definitely matters, none of these guarantee the smooth settlement of your claim. In fact, claim settlement is not in your control.

You have to make full health disclosures to the insurer while buying any policy, you have to involve your family members and educate them on why you are buying this policy and how to claim it whenever and if required, and sometimes even after doing this all, due to some issues the claim gets delayed or repudiated by the company. It happens. May be due to operational Issues, hospital delays or any other reasons. And accepting this will give you peace and calmness to deal and be prepared with such situations.

When looking at a client's cash flow management, I find many people blaming their income for low investible surplus. "Paise bachte hi nahi hai" is the common excuse for people who avoid financial planning. Whereas the important thing to understand is that cash surplus is not the factor of income alone; spending plays an equal role in it. Income is something you can't control and it may take time to reach a decent income bracket, but controlling your spending is in your hand and this is where you should focus on.

Applying Focus on Money Management

The whole exercise of financial planning is all to help you learn about your financial situation, accept it and bring your focus to the important goals you yourself have decided to reach. In short, be good with money to make it be good with you. And in this noisy world, it is quite easy to get distracted from the path, which is why it is advisable to follow a defined process.

If there is no process, then you tend to save haphazardly and without any focus. You start saving for one but withdraw for another, you start for the long term but withdraw after a few years, you invest to provide you income, but keep searching for growth and thus select wrong products. You start with a particular goal like children's education, retirement etc. and put yourself into a process of savings in mutual funds, bank deposits and other suitable products, but after some years start looking for opportunities to withdraw the same. You may come up with many reasons to support your decisions, like you have been told or have read somewhere that this is not a good product to invest in or you bring on some other requirement which was not in your plan like buying a car or some other major expense.

These justifications clearly show your inability to stay focused and be true to your goals. You always get carried away with your desires and forget about your actual need and when instant gratification sets in, you overlook your long-term responsibilities. Your life and money both demand your limited attention. You need to use your time and focus wisely.

Wellness can't be Evaluated in Numbers

"But I am following my financial planner's advice to the T, he is a very good friend of mine, yet my portfolio is in the negative. Why?" Goodu wanted to know.

I consoled him, "Well, there could be 2 reasons to it. One you do not trust your friend as a professional because you have a casual relationship with him, as they say "ghar ki murgi daal barabar", which is why you are asking me about this. Professional advice does not go well in a casual relationship. He can't force you to do something, and you don't need to take his advice seriously. Start paying him his fees and you will start asking him the right questions. Do remember that your friend is your friend first and professional advisor later. So it is better to have a professional by your side who can give you friendly advice.

And the second reason is that your parameters of evaluating your financial planner are wrong. I mean your financial planner may not be solely responsible for your portfolio not getting you high returns. Let me explain with a story.

Two years ago when I joined a gym, my target was to lose 10 kgs of weight. My instructor there laid down an exercise schedule and specifically told me that my target would be achieved by regularly coming and exercising in the gym, and not just by joining the gym. Wasn't it obvious? But still, he preferred to clarify this to me.

Then after a few days, he told me a very strange thing. Yes, it was strange to me. He said that losing weight is about 40% healthy diet, 40% good sleep and 20% right exercise.

This was a kind of a shock to me.

I used to think that only exercising would get me to my goal, but now I had to involve my spouse, ensure that I ate the right food, show discipline in my eating habits, make arrangements in my work schedule and bring some peace into my life to have a good night's sleep.

There are some things where the gym instructor can be of help, but in some, I need the help of other experts.

At the start, I was a bit disappointed, but later on, I realized that **this advice showed me a path of true fitness that I was looking for.**

The realization and understanding on the aspects to work on to reduce my weight comes only by joining a gym and by having a good instructor by my side, from whom I keep receiving the guidance time and again.

I followed the gym instructor's suggestions on exercise, but did not take much effort on my diet and sleep front. Although my weight did not reduce as expected, but the wellness quotient improved as I started feeling more active which improved my otherwise sedentary lifestyle."

You cannot evaluate everything on numbers, especially financial planning by just looking at investment returns. There are many aspects which generally don't get measured like prepaying bad loans, exiting unsuitable policies, following asset allocation which suits your risk profile, the confidence that investor feels having an organized financial life, happiness of goal achievement, estate planning advice etc. Like fitness, financial planning is also 80% behaviour and

20% investment returns.

Goodu was looking confused. I smiled at him, "You must be thinking that does this mean that one should ignore investment returns completely? No, not at all. But how much is the expectation and what should be reasonably assumed should be decided at the time of financial plan preparation. And those assumptions should be accepted only after understanding the definition of the perfect investment portfolio. These numbers can become a base to evaluate the investment returns of the portfolio suggested by the planner.

See, financial planning is like practicing yoga. With yoga you may not look like a body builder but with the stretching and breathing exercises, you will always remain fit and healthy. It's all about wellness."

Goodu suddenly understood, "You're right! Wellness like immunity cannot be measured. It's a feeling. You may not lose 5 kg of weight which you intended to, but to feel fit and active is all that matters. Living rich is more important than getting rich, as the former is internal and the latter may be in comparison!"

The whole purpose of being good with money is to bring wellness in your life.

BEING GOOD WITH MONEY - CONCLUDING THOUGHTS

Being Good With Money - Concluding Thoughts

"I am tired, let's talk tomorrow", "I have been busy all week so I could not think about it", "I have lot of work in office so will not be able to devote time." These are but a few statements you use even when the question in front of you requires your attention and action. The question could be about your health, about your spouse, your family, your personal goals, or even about your work, colleague or a project you are working on.

You want work life balance. But look at both separately and independently of each other. If you do not understand that when your personal life is not in order then your work life will definitely get impacted and when your work is in the doldrums, then how can your personal life be at peace? When things are not going your way, you try to find solace in money, without understanding that money is also a part of your life and not a third person who will come and solve your issues. In fact, it also gets impacted when you are not doing well in any sphere of your life.

A **Rich life** demands you to stay happy and enjoy all that is available to you. It wants you to **be good.** You have to value each of your relationships and work on improving them, make it better time and again. Even money management is a kind of relationship management as the way you treat your money is how it is going to respond to you. Along with skills and time, money management also requires maturity in handling finances.

Maturity is in understanding and questioning your beliefs. Maturity lies in understanding that you are different from your neighbours, friends, colleagues and thus you are not supposed to copy their behaviour and actions. You may learn from them but before applying it to your circumstances, you should know yourself better. Maturity is in accepting that you cannot control anything except your own self.

Being good does not mean you have to or could be able to please everyone, but if you have enough emotional love and care deposits with them, they would understand that you are not being bad or negligent towards them. Being good makes you trustworthy and dependable. Managing relationships require your time, efforts and occasionally skills, so sometimes you need to figure what could be a better and effective way to invest your limited time. Time management is not limited to just your work and relationship management is not limited to your personal life.

If you are managing things well then it should reflect in your life. If you are rich only in money terms but do not have a loving relationship with your spouse or you're always living in stress due to work pressure, what's the point?

I have tried to cover the important aspects which can be applied in all your relationships. Money is something which doesn't ask much time from your side, but due to the super importance given to it, it takes a lot of your time. It can be put in a structure, a system can be developed around it, many parts of its management can be outsourced and then it can be reviewed and monitored timely. The important thing is to understand how you want your financial structure to work and around what goals, as in where you are and where you want to go.

But when you cling so much to money you tend to forget and ignore other areas which only you can manage and expect your time. To keep up your health, only you can walk, jog or gym. Your kids need their parents' time only, no one else can read a book on your behalf, only you are required to go to your work, your spouse needs your time and you cannot outsource any of this. There is nothing wrong in accepting that you are not a Superman. You have to learn saying NO to many things makes saying YES easy to the more important things in your life.

Take charge of your life. Be good. Goodness is keeping your surroundings happy. It's not only about you, it's everything around you. Your Family, your environment, your domestic help, your car washer, your colleagues. When you are good, you help others be good and so we can have a good world to live in and can give a good future to the coming generations.

Good Moneying!!